AN UNLIKELY INTERVENTION

AN UNLIKELY INTERVENTION

A Startup Company's Quest to Conquer
the World's Second Leading Killer of Children

THOMAS WASHING

Published by Leather Apron Media, Avon, Colorado.
www.unlikelyintervention.com

Distributed by Leather Apron Media.
Special discounts are available on quantity purchases by corporations, associations, and others. For details, contact the publisher:
tom@unlikelyintervention.com

DiaResQ is a registered trademark of PanTheryx, Inc.

Library of Congress Control Number: 2018943608

ISBN: 978-1-7321225-0-5 (hardcover)
ISBN: 978-1-7321225-1-2 (paperback)
ISBN: 978-1-7321225-2-9 (ebook)

Editor: David Moldawer
Cover and interior design: Paul Dotey
Cover photograph: Jodie Willard
Author photograph: Sherri Innis

Printed and bound in the United States

A LifeTree Media Book

To Susan

CONTENTS

Introduction

Rashni was dying. Her mother, Pushpa, knew her five-month-old daughter was dying because she had witnessed the suffering and death this affliction caused in dozens of other children in the area. Disease pervaded the slum where they lived, the Bindal Pul area of Dehradun in northern India.

Like most residents in the slums that emerge like weeds along the dried-up riverbeds on the city's periphery, Pushpa and Rashni lived in a dirt-floor shack beneath a sheet-metal roof, with no electricity or running water. Raw sewage and excrement from outdoor defecation, swept down to the riverbed by incessant rain, brought infectious pathogens into the lanes between the shanties.

The contaminated water and bacteria-infested food regularly sickened the slum's youngest inhabitants, whose immune systems were compromised by malnutrition. Rashni had contracted the most dreaded of these diseases—acute infectious diarrhea.

As critical nutrients flushed from Rashni's frail body for the third day in a row, Pushpa knew that, without rehydration therapy from a clinic, her child's life would soon be snuffed out. At sunrise, she knotted a sari around her neck to transport her baby and began walking the narrow, busy streets.

Her destination, seven sweltering miles distant, was the Doon Government Hospital, which operated a diarrhea clinic for the most seriously ill children among the thousands of impoverished families in the Dehradun slums. When Pushpa reached the clinic hours later, the line of parents with stricken children stretched down the hallways and out the door into the oppressive mid-day heat.

Realizing Rashni was near death, nurses rushed her to a table to administer intravenous solutions and antibiotics. The circumstances were dire. For infants as frail and sick as Rashni was, the severe dehydration caused by diarrhea was often deadly. Replenishing vital liquids would help, but it wouldn't stop the diarrhea episode or prevent its recurrence. Even if she survived, each day the episode persisted would increase the likelihood of permanent damage to Rashni's long-term health and development.

Dr. Joshi, the clinic's head physician, approached Pushpa about a pilot study being conducted at the clinic by Bimla Starzl, an Indian-born American nurse. Starzl was testing a food-based powder invented by her husband, Tim. When mixed with water and given to children suffering from acute diarrhea, it had been shown to halt even the most serious diarrhea episodes in hours rather than days. Dr. Joshi had tested the product once before in his clinic, with astonishig results.

After examining the comatose child, however, Bimla concluded that Rashni's condition was too dire to meet the criteria of the study protocol. Knowing the infant was unlikely to survive through the night, Dr. Joshi suggested Bimla administer the powder to Rashni anyway, as a last resort. After conferring with Tim, she agreed and Rashni was given the mixture that evening.

A doctor observing the child around midnight noted she'd begun opening her eyes. By the next morning, Rashni's diarrhea had subsided; she was alert, looking around the room and responding to Pushpa's touch. After examining Rashni on his morning rounds, Dr. Joshi took Bimla aside.

"You saved this child's life."

***

On a late October afternoon in 2010, an email arrived on my computer with a provocative subject line: "PanTheryx Rising." The message, from a longtime business acquaintance, began: "I just wanted to wave my hand in the air as a friend here. Things are heating up at PanTheryx."

Although unaware of the company, I was intrigued. "I think it is an opportunity that has profound implications for doing great good in the world," he wrote. He added that they needed funding.

PanTheryx had been founded by Tim Starzl and his wife, Bimla. I realized I knew Tim, a Boulder, Colorado-based inventor and entrepreneur, from an investment I'd made in one of his companies two decades earlier. Shortly after receiving the email, I met with Tim and Bimla, who had been born in northern India. That was when I learned that Tim had invented and conducted successful tests on an inexpensive, natural, food-based product designed to rapidly halt acute diarrhea episodes in young children.

Since acute diarrhea typically lasts for days or even weeks despite intervention, the potential significance of Tim's invention boggled the mind. For me and almost everyone living in North America or Europe, diarrhea is mostly a nuisance. For much of the rest of the world, the scope and impact of the disease is astounding.

Diarrhea is not only one of the world's most common illnesses but it is also the second leading cause of death among children aged five and under. It exacts a toll greater than the number of childhood deaths caused by AIDS, measles, and malaria *combined*. Only pneumonia kills more children than diarrhea.

Every day in the developing world about 2,200 young children die from diarrheal disease. Annually, it kills over 800,000 children under five, 400,000 in India alone. Diarrhea is also a leading cause of malnutrition and stunting in children under five years old.

The risks are not confined to children. During the twentieth century, more people died from complications of diarrhea than in all wars combined. In the United States, diarrhea episodes exceed 200 million per year. Only the common cold is more ubiquitous.

The World Health Organization (WHO) defines diarrhea as "the passage of three or more loose or liquid stools per day." Although the condition has beleaguered humankind throughout history, it still eludes eradication. The earliest historical evidence of the disease appears in the Neolithic, around 10,000 B.C. As humans transitioned from hunting and gathering to farming, large numbers of people began to live together in communities. This proximity, intensified significantly today, facilitated the transmission of infectious diseases, diarrhea being a prominent example.

After hearing the PanTheryx story in late 2010, I organized and participated in an angel investment round, joined the board of directors, and assisted in recruiting a seasoned management team to build the company. Only as my involvement deepened did I begin to grasp the magnitude of the company's mission. In my 30 years as a venture capitalist working with early-stage companies, PanTheryx was the most audacious undertaking by a startup company I had encountered—an underfunded handful of entrepreneurs setting out to conquer a disease that had plagued humankind for millennia.

As a father and grandfather, I was inspired and deeply touched by the mission of saving infants from the irreparable health effects, or even death, caused by prolonged diarrhea episodes. I'm an investor, not a writer, but, spurred by my passion for the mission and my sense of its potential historic importance, I began to chronicle my experiences working with PanTheryx in 2012.

Why me? Among the many stakeholders—founders, management, employees, and investors—I was one of the few people who had maintained a close working relationship with everyone involved from the outset.

During a family hiking trip in the Atacama Desert of northern Chile in June 2013, I shared the idea of writing this book with my wife, Susan, and teenaged daughter, Taylor. Taylor was to depart Chile shortly to work at an orphanage in the Peruvian Andes, an area where children suffered disproportionally from the disease PanTheryx sought to conquer.

Their support for the project was immediate and effusive. Although only time would tell how the story would unfold, I found on that trip the encouragement I needed to begin shaping my notes into a comprehensive narrative. And our investment in PanTheryx turned out to be part of a trend. Since then, interest in "impact" or "double bottom line" investing that endeavors to generate social benefits as well as financial rewards has gained momentum.

By recounting the story of PanTheryx, I hope to inspire young (and not-so-young) entrepreneurs to consider building companies that "do well by doing good." Each of us has the capacity to use business to improve lives within our communities and across the planet. As musician and activist impact investor Bono commented, "putting profit before people is an unsustainable business model… giving the two equal time is the way forward."

The PanTheryx journey may serve as a template for others seeking to accomplish this goal. The company has already had an amazing impact using the tools of the startup world: inventive genius, out-of-the-box thinking, creative team-building, angel funding, and private equity. The challenges of creating a prosperous company from a startup enterprise will be no less daunting, but the journey, and perhaps the outcome, will be vastly more fulfilling.

One final note regarding the disease that is the antagonist of this story. You may feel that diarrhea is too unpleasant a topic to explore in a book. Unlike malaria or dengue fever, which are easy enough to contemplate in the abstract, diarrhea is something many of us have experienced firsthand. Just remember that being inconvenienced by diarrhea is a far cry from the horrifying prospect that it could kill a child or stunt her long-term growth. I anticipate that, as you read, your familiarity with the condition will breed understanding and hope.

In the end, this book treats a topic of even greater importance than a cure for any individual disease: the vast potential of creative genius and ingenuity when combined with entrepreneurship. In telling the story of how a handful of driven, compassionate, and tenacious people are improving the lives of millions, I hope to open your eyes to the capacity within every entrepreneur to change our world for the better.

1

The Founders

If you look deeply into the palm of your hand, you will see
your parents and all generations of your ancestors...You are
the continuation of each of these people.
—Thich Nhat Hanh, *Present Moment Wonderful Moment*

Tim Starzl's remarkable drive and creativity did not emerge in a
vacuum. Invention, a boundless work ethic, and brazen eccentricity
define several generations of the Starzl family.

R. F. Starzl was the editor and publisher of the *Globe Post*, a
respected, family-owned newspaper in Le Mars, Iowa, not far from
Sioux City in the north-central part of the state. In R. F. Starzl's day
a sign on the edge of town welcomed visitors to "the corn and hog
capital of the world"; Le Mars eventually became home to one of
the world's largest ice cream manufacturing plants and today proudly
declares itself "The Ice Cream Capital of the World."

Starting in the late 1920s, R. F. Starzl wrote science fiction that "envisioned universes within universes down to microscopic size, each with its own sophisticated life organization." Though moderately well-known and an acquaintance of fellow midwesterner Ray Bradbury, Starzl eventually focused his attention on the family newspaper business. Moving on from dreaming up new worlds, Starzl still showed the family knack for invention, conceiving and building an early device capable of photoelectric engraving.

R. F.'s second son, Tom, born in 1926, grew up working in the newspaper print shop. Leaving Le Mars to join the navy after high school, Tom attended Westminster College in Fulton, Missouri, before simultaneously earning his MD and a PhD in neurophysiology at Northwestern, going on to a remarkable career as one of the world's leading organ transplant surgeons. Moving to Colorado in 1962, Dr. Starzl established the organ transplant program at the University of Colorado School of Medicine. Under his leadership, Colorado became the leading center of human kidney transplantation.

Working at the leading edge of medical science, Dr. Starzl faced repeated failure and loss of life, generating controversy. As one writer observed, "The barrage of ridicule and criticism Starzl suffered at the hands of the scientific-medical community at that time was unending." He persevered, however, and in 1967 performed the first successful human liver transplant. As Dr. Starzl's reputation for groundbreaking research and surgical experimentation grew, he moved to the University of Pittsburgh in 1980, where he founded the Pittsburgh Transplantation Institute (eventually renamed the Thomas E. Starzl Transplantation Institute), which became the world's largest organ transplant program.

During his tenure in Pittsburgh, Dr. Starzl was characterized as "one of the world's true eccentrics" with a reputation as "a volatile and unyielding taskmaster." He routinely worked 70- and 80-hour shifts and expected the same grueling work ethic in his fellow surgeons. "The man is an enigma," one colleague said. "He is a person who has an energy quotient that is so far off the scale of most humans that it is almost unbelievable."

Dr. Starzl also emerged as a prolific medical author, described in 1999 by the Institute for Scientific Information as the most cited scientist in the field of clinical medicine. He has been aptly described as "the Father of Modern Transplantation."

Dr. Starzl moved to Denver in 1962 when Tim, his oldest son, was six years old. When I asked Tim to describe life with a workaholic father, he acknowledged that it posed challenges for the family. Yet he himself embraced it. A gifted and restless student, Tim spent as much time as he could with his father, time that was decidedly more interesting than the routine of elementary school.

In fact, the hospital became Tim's educational venue of choice. "My entire childhood was spent there," he said. "I would sleep on the couches, eat in the cafeteria, work on minor clinical things, and go on rounds with the doctors." By the time Tim was nine—and to the dismay of hospital administrators—he was attending autopsies and scrubbing in to his father's surgeries. He was even in the room during the first liver transplants ever attempted.

Dr. Starzl's pioneering work in the 1960s was difficult, complex, and controversial. "This was bleeding edge, experimental surgery involving a completely unknown space," Tim told me. "Nobody knew how to control the immune system, so the process was widely considered impossible to do for fundamental immunological and chemical reasons." Because of the high risks, the presence of so many terminal patients, and the marginal survival rates, Tim recalls the atmosphere of the transplant center as being "brilliant, but extraordinarily grim."

Even as a young man, Tim was keenly aware of his father's international reputation as an iconoclast. Putting efficiency ahead of decorum, he would use a bicycle to navigate the hospital as quickly as possible. He exhibited little regard for the personal lives of those working around him, consistently placing his work above all else. Even on New Year's Eve, when most of the hospital was dark, the lights would be on in the transplant surgery center, operations proceeding as usual. Dr. Starzl's disdain for administrators, protocol, and "the business side" of hospital procedures was palpable. The doctor's unrelenting work ethic, his disregard for authority, the way he sidestepped the accepted way of doing things—none of this was lost on young Tim.

Tim conceded to me that this unusual upbringing gave him a very "different point of view from most people about experimentation, about what is possible, about overcoming obstacles, being smart about solving problems, and doing your homework." Looking back, he recalls the pride he felt in having been permitted to observe a procession of the best and brightest surgeons in the world performing in "one of the most elite medical environments that ever existed, still legendary to this day."

***

After graduating from high school in 1973, Tim enrolled at the University of Colorado, intending to major in molecular biology. After a few years, however, he realized to his surprise that he had little interest in becoming a doctor. In fact, he found himself most drawn to the flexible and inclusive philosophies of Hinduism, Buddhism, Jainism, and Sikhism.

In contrast to Western religious dogma, the Indic religions are nonexclusivist; their believers are welcome to espouse two or more, or selected aspects of each, simultaneously. Tim delighted in the Indic concept that preconceived notions of belief or behavior were by their nature suspect and, therefore, open to challenge and refutation.

Tim's major in Eastern Philosophy led to a master's program in Eastern Strategy and Policy focusing on the *Arthashastra*, an ancient Sanskrit text on political, military, and economic strategy. In the end, however, Tim's pragmatism won out. Assuming—falsely, as it turned out—that a deep understanding of Indian philosophy and religion wouldn't benefit his career, Tim transferred to the business school and graduated with an MBA in 1982.

Within a year of graduation, Tim founded his first company, BioStar Medical Products, in Boulder, Colorado, focusing initially on rapid detection systems for autoimmune diseases. BioStar successfully spun its product line to Corgenix, a diagnostics company based in nearby Broomfield. BioStar's further acquisition of optical technologies from companies in Sweden eventually led to its most celebrated creation, a system platform called Optical Immunoassay (IOA).

BioStar also brought me into the picture. I met Tim in the mid-1980s, when he was pursuing venture capital funding to grow the business based on the IOA platform. IOA's flagship application was one of the first rapid, sensitive strep A tests. With it, physicians would be able to confirm the infection in a few minutes in their offices instead of waiting a day or more for a throat swab culture. I was impressed; my firm participated in several rounds of funding for the company. BioStar went on to be sold in 1998. Today it's a part of Alere, a three-billion-dollar diagnostics company.

Tim's next company, DDx, specialized in detecting biological conditions in food production and agriculture. One DDx system detected pathogens in livestock. Another made it possible for cattle and dairy farmers to identify precisely when cows were in heat, optimizing artificial insemination. This product line, later sold, remains a leading product of its kind in the industry. At one point, the federal government engaged DDx to develop systems for detecting biological warfare agents. In 2001, DDx was sold to Denver-based Acceler8, which later grew to become a $550-million business.

Starzl ingenuity didn't stop with Tim. By the age of 15, when most of his peers were slinging burgers, Tim's precocious son, Ravi, was installing enterprise computer systems for Boulder corporations. Bored with high school, Ravi got his Certificate of General Educational Development (GED) and entered the University of Colorado, where he focused on philosophy, molecular biology, and computer science.

In 1999, Tim partnered with Ravi to found SearchLogic, a company focused on Internet search and email. Ravi left Colorado to work with his dad before transferring to the University of Pittsburgh. Following graduation, he earned his master's and PhD from Carnegie Mellon's prestigious computer science school. Carnegie Mellon immediately recruited him to join the faculty, where he became an expert in the rapidly emerging field of big data analytics.

* * *

By the time he began collaborating with Ravi on SearchLogic, Tim had established a formidable record as an entrepreneur and inventor. Yet, though credited with groundbreaking inventions and patents, Tim hadn't reaped significant financial rewards, even as his products and companies went on to generate millions for others. I asked Tim why it turned out this way. He insisted that, during this stage of his life, his personal motive wasn't money, it was something much more interesting: a question. "Is this an absolutely impossible problem, or can I solve it?"

Of course, Tim would be the first to acknowledge that this impressive career, devoted to innovation over profit, was largely made possible by the support of his wife, herself an extraordinary individual. Bimla Nanka Chand Williams was born in the Meerut District of northern India, part of a Rajput dynasty of royal warriors known as Suryavanshi: "Family of the Sun." The Rajput caste, long dominant both politically and militarily in northern India, is made up of dozens of clans, and its members are often characterized as particularly brave and chivalrous. As the story of PanTheryx progressed, Bimla's warrior lineage would play a pivotal role.

Prior to Bimla's birth in 1950, her grandparents had migrated from the desert city of Jodhpur in the northwest to Meerut, 50 miles northeast of New Delhi, where they acquired large landholdings east of the city. This estate became Bimla's childhood home. Bimla's grandfather had fought with the British army during World War I, in accordance with the Rajput tradition of military service, and the family remained staunchly pro-British throughout her childhood, even adding "Williams" to their Indian name.

Bimla's father was a career military officer who fought in World War II, as well as in India's wars with Pakistan and China. At one point, he was captured and imprisoned by the Chinese during the Sino-Indian Border Conflict of 1962 and was eventually released. Because her father constantly moved from one military theater or camp to another, Bimla and her sister were primarily raised by her grandparents. Bimla recalls a "very privileged" upbringing attending India's finest British boarding schools. She confided to me that her grandmother was her exemplar, "a force to be reckoned with whether you were a family member, a villager, a local bandit, or another powerful clan."

Bimla went on to attend nursing school. While there, her family befriended an oncologist visiting from Denver to pursue his research. He suggested that Bimla continue her nursing studies in an American hospital. Against her family's wishes, the determined 19-year-old boarded a plane to pursue a new life halfway around the globe.

Shortly after she arrived in Colorado, Bimla moved into an apartment building near the University of Colorado Medical Center.

Meanwhile, another new resident was settling in at the opposite end of the floor: Dr. Tom Starzl, finding his footing in the middle of a divorce. Encountering Bimla in the elevator one day, Dr. Starzl promptly suggested she meet his son, Tim, then working as an emergency medical technician and staying with him. The stage was set for an unlikely partnership between the son of a world-famous surgeon and the daughter of a royal family from northern India. Tim and Bimla married the following year.

2

An Unlikely Intervention

Innovation never comes from the established institutions. It's always a graduate student, or a crazy person, or somebody with a great vision.

—Eric Schmidt, former CEO, Google,
former chairman, Alphabet

The man with a new idea is a Crank until the idea succeeds.

—Mark Twain, *The Jumping Frog*

News of Bimla's 1976 marriage was not well received among her sprawling network of Rajput relatives back in India, most notably by her grandmother, who deplored her granddaughter's pairing with an American "white guy." The acrimony in her hometown ran so deep that the Starzls decided to forgo a visit.

Tim and Bimla named their son, born in 1980, Ravi Suryavanshi Starzl. Tempers cooled; the arrival of a male child who would per-petuate the Suryavanshi dynasty persuaded Bimla's grandmother to invite the Starzls to visit India. Tim was cautiously welcomed by the family, especially by the elders, who found themselves impressed by his knowledge of Indic religion and philosophy and his ability to grasp some of the multilayered complexities of Indian culture.

Twenty-five years after this first family reunion, Tim and Bimla contemplated starting a company focused on India's health-care needs. Tim's father had invited them to attend a series of conferences at the University of Pittsburgh Medical School about the future of medicine and emerging health policy initiatives. The discussions highlighted a global shift in demand away from Western-oriented technology and services to solutions for health-care crises in emerging countries.

In 2006, the Starzls traveled to India to investigate business opportunities that might justify the formation of a new company. The following year, encouraged by what they'd seen, they formed PanTheryx. (The reason for the name? It could be pronounced in Hindi, India's most widely spoken language, and it was otherwise innocuous.)

The Starzls envisioned a company that would transfer health-care technology from the West to emerging high-demand markets in the East. The company's officially stated mission at first was to "manufacture and sell a line of branded generic drugs in northern India."

Discussing it with me, Tim described these exploratory trips to India and the field trials that followed as "Indiana Jones stuff." It was a daily adventure confronting ceaseless traffic, stifling pollution, monsoon floods, insufferable heat, and abject poverty. In the winter months, dense fog closed airports and roads and caused deadly train collisions. Bimla described India as "sensory overload all the time, in every way."

Executives visiting the subcontinent on behalf of large pharmaceutical conglomerates travel first-class all the way. The Starzls, in contrast, made visit after visit with the frugality of college students on their first trip abroad—partially to save money, and partially, as Tim put it, "to stay at the same hotels and walk the same streets as our customers."

In New Delhi, they became regulars at Cottage Yes Please, a

budget hotel near the railway station and the main bazaar in the Paharganj district. It was also located in an area largely avoided by American businesspeople due to its reputation for drug trafficking and other illegal activities. The area is evocative of marginal neighborhoods in cities throughout India. Narrow thoroughfares strain to accommodate the crush of street vendors, bicycle taxies, motorcycles, food carts, feral dogs, and pedestrians. A potpourri of laundered saris and apparel dangle above the streets like holiday ornaments among the anarchic jumble of power and telephone lines, as if strategically positioned to distract passersby from the trash and sewage at their feet. During their visits to India, Tim and Bimla acclimated to roaming these streets, mesmerized by the exuberance of the inhabitants and the sensuousness of the setting.

Over time, the Starzls assembled a network of friends and other connections. From high-end legal representation to reliable car drivers, from familiar hotels to contract producers and laborers, the Starzls gradually built up PanTheryx's presence in the country.

Hoping to identify new or untapped health-care opportunities, PanTheryx employed several dozen sales representatives to call on doctors and pharmacies in northern Indian cities. During this process, Keith Brenner, a Boulder businessman who had been providing occasional marketing advice to the company, visited India for the first time to attend his son's wedding. Recalling the experience to me, Brenner remembered his bewilderment upon arriving in a land where "your senses are always being assaulted by something: the noise, the pollution, the colors, the languages." He added, "I don't think it can be understood."

The Starzls, who also happened to be visiting New Delhi, invited Brenner to meet with the new PanTheryx sales team. As he began presenting, Brenner noticed to his chagrin that the salespeople were tilting their heads from side to side, disapproving of everything he said. He later learned that this movement actually signifies something closer to agreement.

Brenner eventually returned to India as PanTheryx's marketing VP, and one of his first requests was that the Indian employees stick to spoken affirmations with him to avoid confusion.

Rather than initially focusing on product development strategies, Tim and Bimla charged their employees with identifying customer needs. They constantly asked doctors the same question: "What is the biggest unsolved problem you encounter on a regular basis?" The dominant response was pediatric infectious diarrhea.

The grim statistics confirmed the doctors' verdict. Despite India's increasing prosperity and economic vitality, the country's population of children less than five years old suffered the highest death rate of any country in the world. Diarrhea caused 13 percent of these deaths, second only to Afghanistan. The only therapeutic treatment available in India, beyond rehydration, was antibiotics. Unfortunately, these were of limited value: they were ineffective with viral infections and regularly overprescribed, killing off beneficial bacteria strains and creating antibiotic-resistant strains of harmful ones.

Tim and Bimla had befriended Dr. Anil Sharma, director of public health for Uttarakhand, a northern Indian state sharing borders with Tibet and Nepal in the Himalayas. Over dinner one night, Tim asked Dr. Sharma why his associates were overprescribing antibiotics for small children when they knew the drugs were not only an unworkable solution for diarrhea but also potentially harmful to the child. "We are using the only tools we have," he replied. "Bring us something better that we can use."

The doctor had posed precisely the kind of challenge Tim exalted in tackling. His mind seized on the question that always drove him: "Is this an absolutely impossible problem, or can I solve it?"

Upon returning to Colorado, "Tim just went crazy," Bimla recalled to me. As his father had done and as he'd done throughout his own career, Tim began working around the clock to formulate an unconventional solution to an intractable problem. Although fully aware of the potential financial rewards and humanitarian benefits, Tim was driven by the challenge above all: "I always find myself more interested in the solving of the problem."

Thanks to their many visits to India, Tim and Bimla were aware of the perplexing mixture of physical, cultural, and environmental factors at play in making pediatric diarrhea so pernicious in the developing world. To be accepted, the product would have to be *simple*: very inexpensive to manufacture, process, and ship, and intuitively effortless to use. It would also need extreme durability, shrugging off cold, heat, and moisture. Unlike vaccines, it could not require refrigeration.

Tim adopted a "garage sale mentality," scouring for "whatever might be lying around that could be aggregated to meet the demand." As he pored over reams of statistical data on pediatric diarrhea in developing countries, one fact captured his attention: children up to six months of age evidenced a substantially lower rate of pediatric diarrhea than children from six months to one year and above.

"I realized that this interesting (and counterintuitive) statistic must be associated with the major biological interaction between mother and child during that time period," he explained to me. "Breastfeeding." Tim also discovered that mothers in India tend to stop or substantially limit breastfeeding after six months. "Unintentionally," Tim told me, "this removed the child's most important orally administered source of acquired immunity leading to a substantial increase in disease." Following this line of reasoning, Tim began to think of remedies for this immunological deficit.

Rather than defaulting to traditional molecular, biologic, or pharmaceutical approaches to bolstering immunity, Tim considered food. An edible remedy would be inexpensive, easy to administer, and, by

its nature, go directly to the location of the problem. The immunological literature he studied was replete with references to colostrum.

Colostrum is a premilk substance produced by all female mammals,
providing the first stage of passive immunity for newborns. Bovine
colostrum has been widely studied for its nutritional and immunological benefits.

In humans, a mother's immune system develops a vast array of
antibodies to neutralize the pathogens acquired from her surround-
ings. While her baby is in utero, all the mother's antibodies pass
through the placenta, transferring a form of passive immunity to the
child. Once the baby is born, many of the mother's immune factors
are selectively excluded from her breast milk. In cows, by contrast,
antibodies do not pass through the placenta. Passive immunity is
passed on in its entirety to the infant calf immediately after birth, in
the form of super-immunized colostrum.

A particularly important antibody contained in abundance in
bovine colostrum, and in only minimal amounts in human breast
milk, is immunoglobulin G (IgG), which is crucial to systemic immunity. In fact, bovine colostrum contains a broad menu of immune
factors beneficial to humans. Tim found two decades of studies
demonstrating that immunoglobulins in bovine colostrum bind themselves to bacteria, viruses, and other pathogens in the gastrointestinal
tract, allowing the immune system to destroy these invaders.

Strangely, colostrum had not been shown to create a material
reduction in the duration of a diarrhea episode. The same went for
antibodies extracted from eggs produced by immunized chickens. In
theory, either of these remedies should have had some impact on
diarrhea, yet neither did alone.

Tim wondered what might happen if these two potent immunological boosters were combined. He theorized that a combination of
bovine colostrum and immune eggs might recreate "the effect of an

immunologically active mother—exposed and reactive to virtually all the diseases that might be affecting the baby." Such a combination might mimic the effect of a mother transferring components of her immune system to her breastfed child, tantamount to, Tim later put it, "loaning an immune system."

As the potential significance of this idea became clear to him, Tim recognized the need to protect his rights to the discovery before sharing the insight with others. In the United States, before filing a full-blown patent application, an inventor has the option of filing a less formal provisional one. Although it wouldn't be reviewed by the patent office, doing so would give him two key advantages before the final application could be filed. First, establishing the date of the invention would be crucial in refuting competing claims. Second, it would allow him to apply the term "patent pending" to the invention.

On November 23, 2009, Tim filed a provisional patent application with the U.S. Patent and Trademark Office: "Method for specifying and creating targeted, broadly reactive immunoreagents and immunotherapeutics and their use in broad-spectrum, undifferentiated, or mixed clinical applications." The application described a broad technology platform for creating a targeted immune response to an invasive bacteria, virus, or parasite.

With the date of the invention protected, Tim turned to the challenge of developing the product. Through an early investor in the company, he was introduced to Dr. Peter Nash, a Minnesota-based microbiologist who had spent the last 30 years developing immunological products for animals, like a product derived from immunized cattle and chickens used to boost the immune systems of calves and piglets. It works by coating the gastrointestinal tract to protect against pathogens for the three weeks it takes for the newborn animal's own immune system to take over.

Dr. Nash's experience immunizing both cattle and chickens to produce antibodies came in handy. Cows are large, difficult to manage, and expensive. Immunized chickens, on the other hand, can be raised by the thousands. They are affordable and easy to manage. Most important, chickens deliver antibodies regularly and predictably, encased in a sturdy, sterile container that's easy to store and handle—an egg.

Discussing Tim's theory with Dr. Nash during my early due diligence investigation of PanTheryx, I was impressed with his deep understanding of the underlying science. Even more notable was his conviction that Tim's notion of combining colostrum with immunized egg material represented a unique concept, never tested in humans, which "could be a big breakthrough."

As an investor, I was fascinated with his suggestion that the product could be a viable alternative to the use of antibiotics in treating not only pediatric diarrhea but also diseases like cholera, dysentery, *Clostridium difficile* (*C. diff*), and clostridium. In fact, Dr. Nash believed such a product might be effective as a prophylactic, dispensed to prevent the occurrence of a diarrhea episode altogether. What Nash described to me represented a revolutionary technology platform with the potential to generate multiple blockbuster therapeutic interventions.

While Tim continued his research, Bimla began tracking down the resources they would need. She met with suppliers. She studied industrial methods of mixing, dosing, and packaging, and methods for maintaining the sanitary conditions needed for manufacturing a food-based product. She also reconnected with Dr. Meg Cattell, a veterinarian with an organic dairy near Fort Collins, Colorado, and an advisor to Tim's earlier company, DDx.

Tim and Bimla convinced Cattell to take on the breeding of a flock of immunized chickens to supply eggs to the company. As a former practicing nurse, Bimla focused particular attention on the sanitation and purity expected of a food-based product.

Improvising a basic production line at the company's office in Boulder, Tim and Bimla dehydrated eggs in a household food dehydrator, ground them up in a coffee grinder, and mixed the resulting powder with off-the-shelf colostrum in a blender. Then they measured the mixture into small, carefully sealed plastic bags.

The prototype was ready. The only question was what to do with it. As founders of a startup company with limited resources seeking to test a product on children in need of it, the Starzls knew they needed to preserve a delicate balance. To keep the company viable, they needed to proceed efficiently and cost-effectively. Meanwhile, they needed to strictly adhere to ethical and medical standards. This may seem like common sense, but international companies had been accused in the past of endangering the health of children in underdeveloped countries by promoting improper products.

The Starzls had taste-tested the product themselves during development to ensure it would be palatable to sick children. (That effort paid off, thankfully. Children enjoy the distinctive milky taste and usually consume it enthusiastically.) Unlike an inherently risky new pharmaceutical compound, a combination of eggs and colostrum could hardly be more benign. To ensure safety, however, Tim and Bimla insisted that the product only be administered together with the standard of care for pediatric diarrhea, including rehydration therapy and antibiotics if recommended by the physician. And, of course, children with suspected allergies to milk or eggs were to be excluded from any study.

Bimla's cousin, a doctor in India, offered to introduce her to Dr. D. P. Joshi, chief of pediatrics at Doon Government Hospital in the northern Indian city of Dehradun. After Dr. Nash reassured Dr. Joshi about the safety of the product, Dr. Joshi agreed to host a trial at Doon hospital. Under the agreement, Dr. Joshi would enroll children in the trial who were under his care and supervision.

As the monsoon season kicked off in June 2010, Bimla left for India with a sufficient supply of the PanTheryx powder. Having grown up near the city of Meerut, 100 miles south of Dehradun, Bimla was familiar with the region and its harsh summer climate. Dehradun, a city of more than half a million people, is located in the Doon Valley, east of the sacred Ganges and near the foothills of the Himalayas. Beginning in late June, the daytime temperature regularly rises above 100 degrees Fahrenheit. With incessant rainfall exceeding 30 inches per month during the monsoon season, it is known as the "Rainy City of India."

The streets of Dehradun teem with traffic of every kind: cars, trucks, bicycles, animals, scooters, and the ubiquitous rickshaws. Pollution drapes the city like a damp blanket. Its government hospital —which provides subsidized health care to the most impoverished families—treats as many as 2,000 patients a day during the monsoon season. Patients largely live in slums that lack refrigeration or clean water. The escalating heat and humidity lead to more contaminated water and bacteria-infested food, which in turn lead to a steady onslaught of acute diarrhea cases.

Bimla described the spectacle she encountered upon entering the hospital as "just plain chaos": throngs of parents and sickly children in lines unfurling in every direction, a stench saturating the cramped waiting rooms. Families from the slums rode public transportation or walked for hours to reach the hospital, which meant the loss of a day's wages. By the time children arrived, most were seriously dehydrated, having endured diarrhea and vomiting for days. More than a quarter of the available beds in the pediatric ward were occupied by these children, some of whom would not survive.

Shortly after her arrival in Dehradun, Bimla met with Dr. Joshi and his associates in the hospital cafeteria. She remembers being a nervous wreck, despite her own experience as a nurse, as she sat down with the medical staff. Dr. Joshi opened the meeting by asking for specific details about the formulation of the product. Bimla cringed internally. Although the provisional patent application had been filed, the exact formulation remained confidential, and for good reason, considering India's notorious disregard for intellectual property laws.

India's drug market, generating annual sales of $12 billion, is one of the country's largest economic sectors—and one of its most corrupt. With over 90,000 different brand names, 90 percent of which are generics, Indian companies sell more than 30 times the number of medical brands sold in the United States or Europe. As if the bewildering array of drugs is not confusing enough, an estimated 20 percent of the drugs sold in India are fakes. One study in New Delhi found that 12 percent of drugs sold in the capital's pharmacies were fake or counterfeit. The report noted: "Some drugs collected for the study from traders were found to contain no active ingredients whatsoever, while other spurious drugs contained chalk or talcum powder mixed with a pain reliever to trick and defraud the patients." Even if fake drugs are identified and the manufacturers are prosecuted, the legal system moves so slowly that the products might continue to be sold for years after charges are brought.

Aware that counterfeiting successful foreign products was all too common in India, Bimla refused to divulge any details about the product or allow the mixture outside of her oversight. All she could do was reassure the Indian doctors that the mixture was absolutely safe. "This was Bimla's gift," Tim later told me, retracing this defining moment for PanTheryx, "her remarkable ability to convince doctors, government agents, and others to do things they realistically should have absolutely no reason to do."

In addition to Bimla's natural persuasiveness, Dr. Tom Starzl's extraordinary reputation in India helped lend the project credibility. The Starzl name carried weight with the doctors of Doon. Eventually, without knowing the product's specific formulation, Dr. Joshi agreed to begin the trial.

Over the next several days, 57 children with serious diarrhea participated in the trial. Twenty-eight were treated with the normal standard of care: oral rehydration supplements and, at a physician's determination, antibiotics. Twenty-nine were given the same standard of care plus the PanTheryx product. At the beginning of each 24-hour period, patients were evaluated for stool frequency, stool consistency, and overall well-being. The results of this admittedly small study were staggering. Twenty-four hours in, children given the PanTheryx product had essentially recovered, while those given only the standard of care had shown virtually no improvement.

Tim, nervously awaiting news back in Boulder, was jolted awake by a phone call in the middle of the night on the second day of the trial. In Dehradun, it was the afternoon following the start of the trial, and Bimla was clearly distressed. Half-awake, Tim struggled to make sense of what she was saying.

As it turned out, Dr. Joshi had refused to record the results for the children who were the most seriously ill when they entered the clinic on the grounds that he simply could not believe the improvement. He feared the data was so anomalous that it might jeopardize his credibility as a physician. In more than 20 years practicing medicine in India, Dr. Joshi had never seen a therapeutic intervention that halted an episode of severe pediatric diarrhea other than antibiotics, which typically required five or six days to work, if they worked at all.

Tim suggested that Bimla ask Dr. Joshi to simply record the results as they appeared and defer any analysis until the program had progressed. Dr. Joshi agreed. With each passing day, everyone in the clinic became increasingly persuaded not only that the product was effective, but also that it was capable of halting even the most severe cases of diarrhea in hours instead of days. As Dr. Joshi witnessed more and more children experience similarly "miraculous results," his attitude evolved from incredulity to curiosity to undisguised fascination.

As parents began returning home with smiling, healthy children, their neighbors began to line up at the hospital with their own children, pleading for access to the same treatment. As she prepared to return to Boulder, Bimla carefully recovered and concealed in her luggage every remaining packet of PanTheryx material.

Weeks after Bimla had returned to Boulder, Dr. Joshi would call asking Bimla if she could send him more packets of the product, lamenting that mothers were standing outside his clinic wanting to know where they could find "the lady from America." Armed with the knowledge that, based on a rudimentary trial at one clinic in India, their invention was effective, safe, and embraced by the patient population it was designed to serve, the Starzls refocused their attention on an equally daunting challenge: how to finance and grow their nascent enterprise.

3

The Leather Apron Club

Virtue in obscurity is rewarded only in heaven. To succeed in this world, you have to be known to people.
—Sonia Sotomayor, *My Beloved World*

I would rather have it said "He lived usefully," than "He died rich."
—Benjamin Franklin

Companies like PanTheryx don't grow through some mysterious force of nature. The right team is crucial. It takes great creativity, a towering work ethic, and perseverance. That said, in my decades working with entrepreneurs and raising money for startup companies, I've identified a distinct factor critical to early-stage growth. The path to creating a successful early-stage enterprise is paved with a matrix of personal relationships. Growth demands a network. The most effective entrepreneurs and early-stage investors rely on personal relationships with trusted, loyal, and supportive people in and beyond their industry. These are peers, colleagues, and collaborators they've worked with for years, even decades. Without this fertile soil of relationships, even the most promising ventures can struggle to take root.

In the case of PanTheryx, long-standing networks nurtured by the founders, investors, and managers played a decisive role. To offer just one example, the email I received alerting me to Tim Starzl's new company came from Dan Arensmeier, a Denver businessman and longtime friend. After encouraging me to look closely at PanTheryx, Dan added that "it would be a great time to have a conversation with Mary about what's going on."

Mary Baum, Dan's wife, was a marketing consultant in the Denver and Boulder business communities. Mary and I had worked on a few projects over the years. When I spoke to her, she immediately offered to arrange a meeting with PanTheryx at her Denver office. On a crisp Colorado morning in early November 2010, I met with Mary and Tim Starzl. We were joined at the table by Tom Schultz, who had been hired as president of PanTheryx a year earlier. Mary had taken up painting alongside her professional career, so the walls of her office featured dozens of her vivid oil paintings.

At that first meeting, Tim projected a warm and loquacious personality. Tech entrepreneurs typically observe an unwritten dress code: khaki pants or jeans, blue, button-down shirt or T-shirt, and flashy athletic shoes. Tim defied the dress code unapologetically. As I would learn from subsequent meetings, you could count on Tim to show up in gray slacks with a white dress shirt, a dark blue sport coat, and black leather shoes.

Tom stood several inches shorter than Tim, with the compact upper body of a weightlifter and a head as spotless as a cue ball. Where Tim was the founder and technical visionary of the company, Tom, a graduate of Johns Hopkins with an MBA from Harvard Business School, ran strategy. Having spent years at a series of consulting firms and early-stage companies, Tom had been hired to infuse PanTheryx with professional management experience.

Tim and Tom recounted the brief history of the company, including the various trips Tim and Bimla had made to India. I was intrigued by the rudimentary yet impressive results from the field trials at the pediatric clinic in northern India. If the trials proved to be credible, they might provide enough validation to raise a new round of funding. Even so, I had my doubts.

Following that initial meeting, I made several reference and due diligence calls. Most confirmed my suspicion that attracting traditional venture capital would be difficult at best. After reviewing the company's business plan, the experts and potential investors I consulted concluded that it simply sounded too good to be true. Reactions hovered between skepticism and incredulity.

I made one of my earliest due diligence calls to an eminent professor of immunology at a major university. He didn't bother to cloak his skepticism. "There really isn't much to say," he told me, "except, this looks sketchy." When I asked him to elaborate, he opined that "the formulation as a mixture of immune factors sounds like snake oil," derisively characterizing the "so-called trials" in India as "a joke" and "pathetic." Hardly an auspicious beginning.

As PanTheryx would learn—repeatedly—going forward, Tim's simple yet profoundly effective invention would find a skeptical audience among doctors and scientists. It often seemed like its very simplicity was part of the problem. Could a treatment lacking any complex, computer-designed molecules cooked up by Big Pharma really work so well on a serious and pervasive illness?

Among investment opportunities, startup investing sits at the high-risk end of the scale, somewhere between Powerball and the Irish Sweepstake. Over 90 percent of startups fail within the first three years. Of the less than 1 percent anointed with an investment from a venture capital firm, 75 percent won't generate a return to their investors.

Worse, as PanTheryx set out to raise capital in 2010, venture capital funding for seed-stage companies of any kind had dropped to historic lows. Investments were still being made, of course, but as an investment PanTheryx faced unique challenges.

To begin with, the quality and experience of the startup's management team is crucial for successful venture investing. The ideal team features many years of relevant experience, proven technological expertise, and compatible entrepreneurs who have worked together on prior ventures and generated attractive financial returns. Prior experience working for a large blue-chip company with an impeccable reputation in the industry makes a great finishing touch.

PanTheryx did not have such a team. While Tim, as chief technical officer, had shown flashes of brilliance as an inventor, he had no technical education. His undergraduate major had been in Eastern Philosophy. Tom Schultz, though an experienced manager, lacked experience working with nutritional foods or at medical technology companies, or running operations in third-world countries. Although each man had spent years working as an entrepreneur with early-stage companies, neither had achieved an exit generating ample financial returns. And Tim and Tom had never worked together before—their compatibility was untested.

Venture firms immediately homed in on these deficiencies. One politely observed that "the team does not have a blue-chip pedigree." A related concern was that three members of the Starzl family—Tim, Bimla, and Ravi—occupied important positions in the company, raising suspicions of nepotism.

The team was just the beginning of the problem. Although venture capital firms are reputedly comfortable with enormous risks, routinely investing in early-stage companies and assuming that only a handful will generate sizable returns, my experience suggests that these investors are actually quite careful, even risk-averse. Venture capital firms focus on specific industry sectors like technology, health care, or retail. Others specialize even further, in subsectors like software, biotechnology, or social networks. There is a general reluctance to invest outside your comfort zone. Firms seek out the types of deals they've invested in previously, often without regard for how successful that approach has been in the past.

Venture capital firms specializing in health-care investments exhibit a strong preference for drugs and medical devices over food-based products. It's a "very tough area," one health-care venture capitalist told me. "A graveyard." This didn't make much sense to me at first. Before drugs and devices can be marketed in the United States, they require Food and Drug Administration (FDA) approval. The arduous approval process involves complex clinical trials entailing years of effort and an outlay of many millions of dollars. PanTheryx's categorization as a food rather than a drug meant that it could go to market without these regulatory approvals. Wouldn't that be an advantage?

It turns out that venture capitalists often prefer products requiring FDA approval because of the hassle and expense. From their perspective, the approval process creates a significant barrier to entry for competing products, conferring a unique market advantage on those with the resources and the patience to go through with it.

The problems didn't stop there. Potential investors were also deterred by the company's target markets. The populations most in need of the PanTheryx solution, though representing potential sales in the billions of dollars, lived in countries variously referred to as "Third World," "emerging," or "underdeveloped." Relatively few startup companies in the United States had successfully launched products into these markets. Those that tried encountered obstacles ranging from opaque bureaucracies to widespread corruption to depressed living standards, all resulting in thin to nonexistent profit margins. These emerging countries also tended to tolerate local pirating of intellectual property from foreign companies. All of this also made a lucrative acquisition by Big Pharma an unlikely prospect. Pharmaceutical companies consider third-world markets unpredictable and price-constrained, so they tend to steer clear.

I suspect that simple logistics also played a role in the resistance we found. Less-developed countries are intimidating propositions for venture firms with little experience operating in remote locations. There are easier ways to put the firm's money to work than boarding an overseas flight to an inhospitable destination to research a potential investment. After enduring a series of negative reactions from prospective investors, I balked. Perhaps the cause was hopeless. PanTheryx was, unquestionably, a high-risk investment, even for a venture capital firm. However, I sensed that it also represented a once-in-a-lifetime opportunity to participate in an effort to solve one of the world's most fearsome health challenges. The mission, and the determination of the founders, inspired me to keep going.

I shifted my focus away from venture capital firms to so-called angel investors. The term "angel investing" traces its roots to wealthy New Yorkers who selectively backed Broadway shows. The term was later adopted to refer to individuals, typically entrepreneurs or executives, willing to risk some portion of their personal wealth investing in early-stage companies. Venture capitalists invest the money of others, and therefore tend to abide by their established investment criteria. Angels, investing their own money, can be a bit more flexible.

While angel investors seek to maximize returns, like any rational investor, they can be enticed by the exhilaration of "being in the chase." In more cases than one might expect, angels will put objective investment criteria aside due to personal enchantment with an exciting new technology or a persuasive entrepreneur (an early enchantment that usually subsides as the investment's prospects dim).

PanTheryx represented what angels consider a "social impact" or "double bottom line" investment opportunity, one "producing social as well as financial returns." One aspect of angel investing that tends to compete with pure objectivity is the opportunity to invest with the goal of "doing well by doing good," a phrase attributed to Benjamin Franklin.

In his biography of the Founding Father, Walter Isaacson recounts that Franklin assembled a group of fellow Philadelphia businessmen to meet regularly and discuss civic improvement projects. A printer by trade, Franklin would wear a leather apron while working in his shop. Seizing on the garment as an apt symbol of industrious pursuit, he dubbed this civic-minded group the Leather Apron Club. Franklin's Leather Apron Club "discussed civic and political issues, devised schemes for self-improvement and formed a network dedicated to 'doing well by doing good.'" Its members were instrumental in launching diverse civic associations "including militia and street-sweeping corps, volunteer firefighters, tax-supported neighborhood constables, health and life insurance groups, a library, a hospital, an academy for educating youth, a society for sharing scientific informa-tion and a postal system to help connect everyone."

Though many American investors since Franklin's time have mixed altruism with prudent investment strategy, the practice has gained momentum with angel investors over the past decade. In May 2012, *The Economist* described a meeting in Santa Barbara, California, of the Giving Pledge Club, a group of billionaires recruited by Warren Buffett and Bill Gates who had each pledged to donate at least half their fortune to charity. The "hottest topic" at the meeting was "impact investing," the challenge of investing "to make a profit and do good at the same time." Although the topic generated great enthusiasm among attendees, Buffett was reportedly "skeptical about the idea," advocating for the separation of business and charity as two distinct endeavors with contradictory objectives. "I think it's tough to serve two masters," he said. "I would rather have the investment produce the capital and then have an organization totally focused on the philanthropic aspects."

In March 2014, "an elite group of 100 young philanthropists and heirs to billionaire family fortunes" were invited to the White House to discuss ways in which the public and private sectors might collaborate to solve society's most pressing issues. Once again, "the topic that seemed to generate intense interest among the wealthy heirs was impact investing, which refers to a socially conscious form of investing that seeks to generate both a social benefit and a meaningful financial return." One of the young heirs emphasized, "We want 100 percent of our assets to be value aligned or impact invested."

With this trend in mind, I began combing through my personal network for potential angel investors to pitch on behalf of PanTheryx. Inspired by Franklin's example, I sought out people who were wealthy, sophisticated, astute, and, importantly, agreeable to hang out with. In other words, I was intent on creating a PanTheryx Leather Apron Club.

Two of the earliest angels I contacted readily satisfied my "agreeable to hang out with" criterion: close friends from college who had joined me in earlier angel investments. Each of the other angel investors I approached had started or managed an early-stage company themselves and created significant personal wealth in the process. They also shared an interest in supporting philanthropic causes, particularly those targeted at helping underprivileged people.

From the founding of the company in early 2007 until my initial meeting with the team in 2010, PanTheryx had raised about one million dollars in modest increments from 38 individuals in the Starzls' network. Those financial resources had essentially been depleted.

Within two months of that meeting, I negotiated a term sheet with PanTheryx's management—on behalf of the founders of the new Leather Apron Club—calling for an angel investment round of up to one million dollars at a price of $1.20 per share, valuing the company at $4.35 million.

The Leather Apron Club term sheet called for an initial investment of $180,000 on December 31 followed by a second investment of $270,000 by February 9, 2011, subject to one important condition. By that date, the company would need to have repeated the first trial and achieve "substantially comparable" results. This meant the next trial would have to be performed in the same location, with the same number of patients, and achieve similarly positive outcomes.

In offering this deal, the Leather Apron Club made a wager that turned a hallmark of early-stage investing on its head: Could an American startup company successfully launch an unorthodox product in the underdeveloped world before proving its value in Western consumer markets?

The founders agreed to the term sheet, committing to decode a puzzle that had perplexed the medical and scientific communities of the world for centuries. Thus, the founders and the investors linked arms, beginning a journey into uncharted territory.

4

A Neglected Disease

For every child in underdeveloped countries, the most important time is today. Each additional day they live increases their chances of reaching adulthood.
— Dr. Mark Grabowsky,
Chief Medical Officer, PanTheryx

There is interest in identifying an alternative source of antibodies which is inexpensive, easy to produce, and safe.
— Dr. Shafiqul A. Sarker et al.
Pediatric Infectious Disease Journal, 1998

Prior to 1970, diarrhea was the world's leading killer of children. Over the past four decades, steady advances in sanitation and hygiene practices in third-world countries and improved treatment methods have dramatically lowered the number of episodes as well as the attendant mortality rate. By 2010 diarrhea was the second leading cause of death among children under five, the actual number of such deaths each year having declined from five million in 1980 to approximately 800,000. These advances are obscured by the enduring scope and complexity of the problem: 1.7 billion episodes of diarrheal disease in children five or younger every year, 36 million of which are classified as severe and, therefore, life-threatening.

As staggering as these numbers are, they may be understating the problem. It's extraordinarily challenging to collect accurate data from remote medical facilities and small villages in underdeveloped countries in Africa and Asia, where the majority of pediatric diarrhea cases occur. As a result, reports evaluating the incidence of diarrheal disease and related mortality rates must be taken with a grain of salt.

Indeed, fewer than half of all deaths globally are properly captured and recorded by competent civil organizations. For instance, of the estimated nine million individuals who die in India every year, most die at home or in rural areas where their deaths are never officially recorded.

Meanwhile, though the official statistics have slowly improved for decades, that trend is projected to reverse. The expected increase in ambient temperatures, flooding, crop failures, and malnutrition in the poorest countries due to climate change threatens to accelerate the incidence of acute cases of pediatric diarrhea. Studies suggest that the number of malnourished children globally will increase 20 percent by 2050 because of climate change. In other words, without an innovative new intervention like the product PanTheryx was introducing, diarrhea would continue to plague children in undeveloped countries indefinitely.

Despite the evidence of its widespread lethal impact on children in the underdeveloped world, diarrhea and its causes and consequences provoke minimal interest in Europe and North America. There, thanks to clean water and safe food, the disease is considered an annoyance rather than a serious killer worthy of investigation.

Imagine a city in the United States admitting that one in every five children under the age of five is dying from something completely preventable. A media firestorm would ensue. Outraged politicians and health-care officials would demand decisive action to address the calamity immediately. This grim scenario has played out for decades across underdeveloped countries and continues to be met with indifference in the developed world. Ultimately, there is an ongoing crisis in countries that lack the wherewithal to address the illness that remains ignored by countries with more than adequate resources to end it.

This disparity was highlighted by UNICEF in a 2012 report on the devastating impact of pneumonia and diarrhea on the world's children. The report concluded that, by 2015, "more than two million child deaths could be averted if national coverage of cost-effective interventions for pneumonia and diarrhea were raised to the level of the richest 20 per cent in the highest mortality countries."

While the UNICEF report acknowledged that enormous progress has been made, "thanks mostly to rapid expansion of basic public health and nutrition interventions, such as immunization, breastfeeding and safe drinking water," it stressed the need for *low-cost curative interventions* against diarrhea and pneumonia. It was the very call to action that had catalyzed Tim Starzl to begin work on his invention.

Diarrhea is not, of course, confined to underdeveloped countries. There are 170 million cases of acute diarrhea in adults in the United States every year. Approximately half of these cases are caused by noroviruses found in contaminated food, frequently taking place in "closed populations" such as cruise ships, nursing homes, dormitories, and hospitals. The health-care costs associated with norovirus cases in the United States alone exceeds $270 million annually. The total annual cost when you add in lost productivity surpasses $5.5 billion.

Approximately 48 million episodes of diarrhea strike children aged five and under in the United States every year. Thanks to safe drinking water, carefully regulated food quality standards, and high levels of sanitation, infectious diarrhea generally isn't life-threatening for children in the developed world. For the same reasons, adults in these countries normally suffer the problem only when they ingest contaminated food or venture into less sanitary environments.

One familiar example of the condition is so-called wilderness diarrhea, afflicting backpackers and campers who make the mistake of drinking untreated stream or surface water. Although this infection, most commonly attributed to the protozoa *Giardia*, can be excruciatingly unpleasant for a few days, especially if you're stuck in the woods, it's not considered life-threatening.

The most recurrent malady affecting travelers from developed countries is commonly known as travelers' diarrhea. As many as 10 million international travelers are affected by it each year, principally those vacationing or traveling on business in the underdeveloped countries of Africa, Asia, and Central and South America, where childhood deaths from diarrhea are endemic. Studies suggest that over 60 percent of travelers visiting tropical and subtropical regions will develop diarrhea.

This fact is instructive. Adults visiting these countries encounter and ingest the same pathogens that trigger diarrhea in indigenous children, suffering the same consequences for the same fundamental reason. The immune system is incapable of quickly defending the body from the pathogenic invaders. In the case of foreign travelers, this is because they have never encountered these particular pathogens before. In the case of local children, it is because their undernourished bodies and immature immune systems are too weak. The travelers suffer an inconvenience for a few days of their vacation. The children all too often don't survive.

In addition to hikers, travelers, and children, soldiers have always been vulnerable. Prior to World War II and the introduction of antibiotics to the battlefield, infectious diseases, most notably diarrhea, killed or disabled more soldiers than combat did. Nearly 45,000 Union soldiers in the American Civil War died of diarrhea or dysentery, equaling almost one-half of the 110,000 killed in combat. Today,

American military personnel are routinely deployed to underdeveloped countries or hostile environments bereft of sanitation. In contrast to leisure travelers, military personnel are stationed in dangerous, inhospitable locations for extended periods of time, performing demanding, high-exertion tasks for weeks on end. Being stricken with acute diarrheal disease in this environment is a terrifying prospect.

Dr. David O. Matson at the Infectious Diseases Section of the Center for Pediatric Research in Norfolk, Virginia, writes: "I expect that our imaginations cannot fathom the problems attendant from the absolute urgency for relief from explosive vomiting and diarrhea when experienced within an armored vehicle under fire and at ambient temperature" of over 100 degrees. The approximately two million military personnel deployed in Iraq and Afghanistan from 2001 through 2007 suffered nearly four million cases of diarrhea, encompassing over 11 million days, causing over one million duty days lost. The attendant misery of the personnel cannot be documented.

***

Although it is commonly referred to as a disease, acute diarrhea is a symptom of an infection in the intestinal tract caused by the ingestion of food or water contaminated with pathogens—microorganisms that cause infection or disease. The pathogens most commonly associated with diarrhea include bacterial, viral, and parasitic organisms.

In July 2013, *The Lancet* published the results of an international study financed by the Bill and Melinda Gates Foundation. It evaluated more than 22,000 children in seven African and Asian countries over a three-year period to determine the pathogens most commonly responsible for severe diarrhea in children. The Global Enteric Multicenter Study (GEMS) was the "largest, most comprehensive study of childhood diarrheal diseases ever conducted in developing country settings." GEMS research revealed that most severe diarrhea cases are caused by one of just four pathogens. The leading cause is rotavirus, followed by *Cryptosporidium* (Crypto; a microscopic parasite), *Shigella,* and enterotoxigenic *E. coli,* the latter two being common types of bacteria.

Rotavirus, the leading cause of severe and fatal diarrhea, accounts for 140 million cases of diarrhea worldwide in children six months to two years of age, leading to the deaths of as many as 600,000 children each year, many of whom would survive with access to adequate hospital care. More children throughout the world are hospitalized due to rotavirus than from any other disease.

Though healthy children in developed countries suffer occasional diarrhea with no long-term consequences, children in low-income countries suffering repeated episodes of diarrhea in a single year risk long-term damage. Studies have shown that during the first two years of life, each day of diarrhea experienced by a child dramatically increases the likelihood of stunted growth, which, in turn, leads to long-term nutritional deficit and decreased cognitive function.

Largely unseen in the developed world, stunting, or being undersized for one's age, constitutes a significant obstacle to human development worldwide. Repeated episodes of diarrhea are a leading cause of malnutrition and, in turn, a primary cause of stunting. Affecting approximately 162 million children around the globe, stunting is irreversible, and its long-term effects are devastating: "diminished cognitive and physical development, reduced productive capacity and poor health, and an increased risk of degenerative diseases such as diabetes," according to WHO. Stunted children grow up to have less schooling, lower test scores, and a greater likelihood of living in poverty. Stunted children are estimated to earn 20 percent less as adults than nonstunted individuals.

The GEMS study confirmed earlier studies, as well as anecdotal evidence, suggesting that the lack of a therapeutic solution capable of quickly shutting down a diarrheal episode often leads to irreparable short- as well as long-term damage to the child. Further, children diagnosed with moderate to severe diarrhea experience more than an eight-fold increase in risk of death over a two-month follow-up period.

A uniquely menacing aspect of pediatric infectious diarrhea is its sinister interrelationship with malnutrition. WHO has reported that 50 percent of malnutrition is associated with repeated diarrhea. Malnutrition is the cause of 53 percent of all childhood deaths and over 60 percent of these deaths among children less than five years of age are caused by diarrhea.

Malnutrition weakens the child's immune system, not only intensifying and prolonging the diarrheal episode but also increasing the likelihood of further and more frequent occurrences. The repeated infections associated with the diarrhea, in turn, inhibit the ability of the mucosal linings of the intestine to absorb nutrients, perpetuating the vicious cycle and resulting in permanent physical impairment or death. Recent studies show these long-term effects to include heart disease, stroke, diabetes, and even obesity, which may help explain the global epidemic of the latter.

Diarrhea also has an economic cost in impoverished underdeveloped countries, where the average per capita income is commonly less than $10 a day. The annual health-related economic impact of diarrhea (including premature mortality, productivity loss, and health-care costs) is estimated at $25 billion dollars in India, $2.3 billion in Bangladesh, and $2 billion in Indonesia.

Pediatric diarrhea also has an economic impact at the family level. To understand how devastating even one case of acute diarrhea can be to a family, you have to tally not only out-of-pocket costs like medicine, doctors, transportation, and diapers, but also indirect costs such as lost wages. A 2008 study in India, where the per capita daily income averages about $10, concluded that a typical household incurs a cost for each diarrheal episode equal to roughly 3 to 6 percent of its *annual* income. More than 80 percent of lower-income families have to borrow money to pay the out-of-pocket costs.

A similar 2013 study in Bolivia could apply to families in any of a dozen underdeveloped countries who are surviving on a small budget and spending over 60 percent of income on food and fuel (leaving little extra for health care, education, and housing expenses). The study concludes that "the cumulative economic impact of multiple diarrheal episodes may devastate a household's overall financial well-being."

***

Prevention of diarrhea is directly related to the availability of safe and sanitary water and hygiene systems. Interventions to improve water quality in underdeveloped countries have been shown to reduce morbidity from diarrhea in children by 42 percent. Thanks to sustained efforts across the globe, amazing improvements have been made in that direction. Since 1990, 2.6 billion people have gained access to improved drinking water and 2.1 billion have gained access to improved sanitation, according to WHO.

Even with such progress, however, over 660 million still lacked access to improved drinking water and 2.4 billion lacked improved sanitation as of 2015. This ongoing lack of sanitary drinking water and food in the underdeveloped world remains the leading cause of diarrhea and malnutrition.

In many countries, cultural beliefs foster a reluctance to improve sanitation. Nowhere is this more apparent than in India where, as recently as 2014, half the population, over 600 million people, routinely defecated out of doors and modern waste treatment systems were virtually nonexistent. In destitute rural areas, latrines are sparse or simply ignored. The predicament is especially acute for women, who are relegated to wandering into fields to squat, with attendant risk of infection or assault. The consequent flow of human waste into parks, rivers, and roads contaminates food and drinking water. The resulting infectious diarrhea problem is so widespread that malnutrition and stunting of growth in young children is even seen in as many as one-third of the country's richest families. In 2014, Prime Minister Narendra Modi launched a program to bring clean toilets to rural areas. "We are in the twenty-first century and yet there is still no dignity for women as they go out in the open to defecate," he said. "Can you imagine the number of problems they have to face because of this?" The project, Clean India, aims to end open defecation in India by installing 75 million new public toilets throughout the country by 2019.

Political promises aside, it remains unrealistic to eliminate unsafe drinking water in underdeveloped countries in the foreseeable future. WHO studies suggest that infrastructure investments worth approximately $535 billion would be needed to bring sanitary drinking water to underdeveloped countries throughout the world.

Prevention of diarrhea is also facilitated by the increasing availability of vaccines designed to address specific causes of diarrhea. The Bill and Melinda Gates Foundation has invested tens of millions of dollars in pursuit of viable vaccine solutions, and estimates that existing vaccines for rotavirus, cholera, and typhoid could dramatically reduce child deaths due to enteric and diarrheal diseases. As effective and promising as vaccines might be, however, they underscore the challenges posed by the realities of the underdeveloped world.

Four vaccines for rotavirus are currently available on the global market. These vaccines are expected to reduce rotavirus-related diarrhea cases by about 55 percent in infants less than one year of age, meaning that about 45 percent of children vaccinated would remain unprotected. These vaccines require either two or three doses, which must be administered a minimum of four weeks apart, posing a logistical challenge for families in rural areas with no nearby clinics or doctors. Further, although rotavirus is the leading cause of pediatric diarrhea worldwide, it is just one of many types of pathogens, including several different types of protozoa and bacteria, responsible for infectious diarrhea. No available vaccine offers a broad-spectrum solution addressing multiple pathogens.

The retail cost of rotavirus vaccines sold on the open market by pharmaceutical companies can easily reach $40 or more per dose, rendering them prohibitively expensive for children in the countries where they are most needed. Subsidies provided by nongovernmental organizations (NGOs) and groups like the Global Alliance for Vaccine Initiative can bring the cost down to two dollars per dose in the most indigent countries, but even that sum can be difficult for poor families.

Underdeveloped countries also pose challenges to effective distribution and administration of most vaccines. Of the four rotavirus vaccines on the market, only Rotasil can stay unrefrigerated for up to six months. One of the vaccines on the market must be stored frozen, and two others require constant refrigeration at temperatures between 35 and 46 degrees Fahrenheit. As more vaccines are introduced in the future, the bottlenecks created by supply chains required to safely transport cold vaccines from the manufacturer to the patient will present ever greater challenges.

Electricity is either unavailable or erratic in underdeveloped countries, epitomized by the July 2012 blackout in northern India that affected 620 million people, including many in the area's largest cities. The unreliability of electrical power, notably in remote areas, precludes the constant refrigeration of vaccines prior to use in the very environments where they are most needed.

***

"Can you name a miracle food that is universally available, free, and can save children's lives and maybe even make them smarter?" asked columnist Nicholas Kristof in a 2013 opinion piece in the *New York Times*. The answer was another preventive measure, capable of substantially reducing deaths caused by diarrhea: breastfeeding.

Born with immature immune systems, infants are highly susceptible to infection from the pathogenic organisms surrounding them from the moment of birth. The mother, having been exposed to indigenous pathogens throughout her life, possesses immunity protecting her from these organisms thanks to the "memory cells" residing in her adaptive immune system. This means that the mother's immune system is constantly producing antibodies to the very pathogens that threaten her newborn child. Breastfeeding allows her to supplement the child's immature immune system, transmitting the antibodies she is producing internally to protect against the infectious causes of diarrhea.

The immunological, economic, social, psychological, and environmental benefits of breastfeeding are stunning, and stunningly underappreciated. One recent study conducted over a 30-year period concluded that breastfeeding for 12 months or longer in early childhood results in higher IQ scores, more years of education, and higher monthly incomes compared to those who are breastfed for less than one month. Studies in Bangladesh reveal that infants who are not breastfed, or only partially breastfed, are four times more likely to die from diarrhea than infants fed exclusively with breast milk.

Marginal breastfeeding results in more than 820,000 child deaths every year. Recent studies conclude that half of all childhood diarrhea episodes and 72 percent of all hospital admissions due to diarrhea could be avoided by breastfeeding. Even in the United States, children of mothers who stop breastfeeding prior to 6 months of age have a significantly greater risk of suffering from diarrhea from 7 to 12 months of age.

International standards now suggest that mothers begin breast-feeding at birth, provide breastfeeding exclusively for 6 months, and continue breastfeeding along with complementary foods through 18 months. Tragically, many mothers throughout the underdeveloped world, unaware of or unwilling to adhere to this standard, suffer a preventable loss of their infant children.

***

With all this discussion of pathogens and weak immune systems, it's important to note that not all microorganisms are bad. The human gut (stomach, large intestine, and small intestine) contains over 400 different species of bacteria, many of which work in harmony with ordinary cells to promote the normal development of the body's digestive and immune systems. Living microorganisms that, when administered in adequate amounts, confer a health benefit on the host are called "probiotics." Several studies in recent years have concluded that these probiotics, if ingested in sufficient quantity, may be effective in preventing or treating diarrhea in children.

The growing fascination with functional food products in developed countries has generated interest in products containing probiotics. In 2016, the global market for probiotics was nearly $36 million. Most of these products are sold in the form of probiotic-containing dietary supplements, yogurts, or other dairy products claiming to "support digestive and intestinal health."

In recent years, WHO has tracked dozens of studies seeking to gauge the effectiveness of probiotics in treating pediatric diarrhea, most conducted in underdeveloped countries. In well-nourished children, the results have been somewhat positive, showing modest decreases in the frequency and duration of severe diarrhea. However, for malnourished children, "the findings were mixed."

Although probiotics are likely to be the continuing focus of attention and controversy, for the immediate future there is no indication that they will have a significant impact in saving the lives of children in the underdeveloped world. Prevention will remain an essential goal in the battle to eradicate pediatric diarrhea. If one accepts the reality that known preventive measures will require decades to reach fruition, short- and long-term therapeutic solutions assume a critical role in fighting pediatric diarrhea in the developing world.

***

To comprehend the extraordinary significance of the PanTheryx solution, you need a brief overview of the available treatments and solutions most widely employed in underdeveloped countries today as well as the relative efficacy and shortcomings of each. Diarrhea has been designated a "neglected disease," defined as an infectious condition that disproportionally affects the poor, especially children, in low- and middle-income countries, with little or no presence in high-income countries. Further, it stands in need of an intervention that is both affordable and can be used "under difficult and health-infrastructure-poor circumstances."

The cost to a pharmaceutical company of developing a new drug can range up to $2.6 billion. The Center for Global Development notes that the development of new treatments for neglected diseases has been minimal "because most people who suffer from them are desperately poor." Diarrheal disease appears on every list of the top 10 causes of death in the developing world, but it is notably absent from an equivalent list for rich countries. The center concludes that, since "drug development for neglected diseases may often be just as expensive and uncertain as it is for diseases that affect the affluent, the interest of pharmaceutical firms in investing in neglected diseases has been understandably small."

Charles Kenny, in his 2013 book *Getting Better,* highlights the problem in graphic terms: "Why consider researching a vaccine for a disease that infects people who spend ten or twenty dollars a year on health care when people in the United States are spending nearly six thousand dollars a year?" Kenny notes that the typical American pharmaceutical company spends more than twice as much on marketing and administration as it does on research and development.

Studies by the George Institute for International Health, funded by the Bill and Melinda Gates Foundation, have focused attention on research and development expenditures directed toward solutions for the most burdensome diseases plaguing third-world countries. Designating diarrhea as one of 30 "neglected diseases," these studies document a shocking disparity in funding for diarrhea cures compared with other, less catastrophic diseases.

The studies concluded that potential cures for pneumonia and diarrhea illnesses, the number one and two killers of children under five worldwide, accounted for only 6 percent of total pharmaceutical research and development expenditures. HIV, tuberculosis, and malaria, which combined have a total disease burden just 75 percent of the burden of pneumonia and diarrhea, received nearly 80 percent of total funding.

Another study surveyed all new therapeutic products introduced from 2000 through 2011 for 49 neglected diseases, all of which are described as "diseases of poverty" concentrated in the world's poorest countries. Of 850 new therapeutic products brought to market for all diseases during that period, only 37, or 4 percent, were aimed at neglected diseases. Less than 1 percent represented potential treatments for diarrheal disease. By contrast, 134, or 16 percent, represented new treatments for neuropsychiatric disorders, a problem decidedly focused on first-world countries. The study found that in 2010, only 1 percent of all research and development spending for global health was allocated to neglected diseases.

Children suffering from chronic diarrhea in underdeveloped countries suffer for days or even weeks for lack of a fast-acting solution to the disease. When the condition persists for even a day or two, fluids and electrolytes drain from the body so quickly that severe dehydration ensues, often leading to death, particularly in infants who are malnourished or whose immune systems are compromised. The only effective response to preclude this tragic result is to swiftly replace the vanishing liquids.

In the early twentieth century, the concept of rehydrating the body intravenously was introduced and found to be effective. Unfortunately, intravenous (IV) fluid therapy required elaborate, sanitized equipment and supplies as well as trained personnel, normally available only in a hospital setting, rendering it too expensive and impractical for widespread implementation in rural areas and underdeveloped countries.

Measurable advances in the use of oral rehydration solutions (ORS) began in the 1950s with the discovery that glucose, mixed with water and salt, enhanced the absorption of liquids into the walls of the intestine. These discoveries emerged from the Pakistan-SEATO Cholera Research Laboratory, later renamed the International Centre for Diarrhoeal Disease Research, Bangladesh (icddr,b), in Dhaka, the capital.

By the late 1960s, scientists at icddr,b, led by Dr. Norbert Hirschhorn, a young American military doctor assigned to the United

States Public Health Service, formulated a groundbreaking regimen of ORS and continuous replacement of lost fluid. The mixture was eventually called oral rehydration therapy (ORT) and led to successful clinical trials of ORT in 1968.

The administration of ORS beginning at the early stages of a diarrhea episode has been estimated to reduce diarrhea mortality by nearly 70 percent. Since the discovery of ORS in the 1960s, it has saved over 50 million lives worldwide. In 1978, *The Lancet* called ORS "potentially the most important medical advance" of the twentieth century. In 2001, the Gates Foundation gave icddr,b its Award for Global Health for its role in the creation and distribution of ORS in Bangladesh.

Zinc has also emerged as a possible treatment. A 10- to 14-day course of zinc can result in a 25 percent reduction in the duration of a diarrhea episode and a 30 percent reduction in stool output, and it helps prevent recurrence for up to three months. Once again, icddr,b, with assistance from the Gates Foundation, was the forerunner in creating the first national rollout of zinc products to the population of Bangladesh.

Zinc alone, however, does not have a material impact on the morbidity rate for infants with acute diarrhea. In recent years, zinc supplements have been added to the recommended regimen for treating pediatric diarrhea. This combination of ORS and zinc supplements became widely regarded as the standard for treatment of acute pediatric diarrhea throughout the world. Keep in mind, however, that this treatment fails to address the cause of the problem—the virus, bacteria, or pathogen—or to halt the diarrhea episode.

Antibiotics have demonstrated limited effectiveness in treating pediatric diarrhea. They are expensive and difficult to transport and store in many regions, and have no effect on viruses, including the leading cause of pediatric diarrhea, rotavirus. UNICEF warns that antibiotics and anti-diarrheal medications are "less effective" than ORT and "should not be routinely administered."

According to PATH, an international health organization, one explanation for this is that "although ORS is a reliable treatment for reversing dehydration, its benefits are not immediately perceptible to caregivers. Seeing no change in a child's diarrhea, caregivers may select other treatment, such as antibiotics, which do not rehydrate, have limited effectiveness, and contribute to antibiotic resistance."

Further, anti-diarrheal drugs and over-the-counter remedies have been generally deemed useless, even dangerous, in treating pediatric diarrhea. PATH reports that if ORS could be accessed and used by all caregivers, "diarrhea deaths would drop by a staggering 93 percent." Despite massive efforts to distribute ORS and zinc to third-world countries, ORS reaches less than 40 percent of children suffering from diarrhea. Involving the ingestion of substantial amounts of liquid and food over an extended period, the treatment, paradoxically, encounters fierce resistance from parents in many parts of the underdeveloped world.

Dr. Atul Gawande, surgeon, best-selling author, and professor at the Harvard School of Public Health, portrayed the dilemma vividly: "To understand why, you have to imagine having a child throwing up and pouring out diarrhea like you've never seen before. Making her drink seems only to provoke more vomiting. Chasing the emesis and the diarrhea seems both torturous and futile. Many people's natural inclination is to not feed the child anything." Stated another way, caregivers want a solution that stops the diarrhea episode quickly rather than a palliative that merely hydrates the child.

A broad survey encompassing 45 countries worldwide has found that children who are denied fluids during diarrhea episodes, typically due to the parents' not having been educated in the associated risk, have a 15 percent greater chance of dying from the disease than children who are properly hydrated.

Notwithstanding the extraordinary success of ORS and zinc at rehydrating the body and accelerating overall improvement in the patient's condition, the combination does not kill the pathogens causing the diarrhea or prevent nutritional morbidity. A 1998 study at icddr,b concluded: "Oral rehydration therapy (ORT), although effective in management or prevention of dehydration, does not reduce the duration or severity of illness. Hence, there is a need for new interventions to further improve therapy for gastrointestinal (GI) tract infections."

Experts around the globe have repeatedly avowed that the holy grail would be a therapeutic intervention that could be administered at home and halt the diarrheal episode in a matter of hours, rather than days. Equally important, this ideal treatment would be a "broad-spectrum" solution, able to cure diarrhea episodes caused by multiple types of pathogens without a precise diagnosis in advance.

The PanTheryx product, eventually branded DiaResQ, represented just such an intervention. Unlike any other remedy ever developed, in most cases it extinguished the pathogens causing the problem and shut down the diarrhea episode in hours rather than days. At this point in the story, the larger question remained: Could the company muster the personnel and financial resources necessary to produce the product in huge quantities and distribute it to millions of waiting patients in remote corners of the earth?

5

"Comparable Results"

In India, people get things done for you if they "like you."
The art is to pull the right string of people and relationships
into line in order to accomplish your objective.

—Tim Starzl

Early-stage companies invariably launch with grand aspirations of rapid growth and prosperity. All too often, however, their trajectories are punctuated by a series of unanticipated obstacles. Early-stage management teams are judged by their ability to see and overcome these obstacles. PanTheryx and its management team were no exception.

Planning around the unpredictable arrival of capital infusions during PanTheryx's early years was a puzzle with many moving parts. The company struggled through ambiguous regulatory, clinical, and scientific challenges, while remaining alert to competition and safeguarding intellectual property and trade secrets, and while recruiting and retaining key employees. Month after month, bureaucratic decisions were delayed, clinical trials were extended, patent applications languished, and corporate partner discussions dragged on. Overshadowing this chaos was the quandary of the ever-dwindling cash balance.

From my perspective as an investor and a director, these early years felt like a demonic game of soccer in which the referee repeatedly extended the goal line, the clock ticking down to the moment when cash reserves were exhausted, and the whistle sounded. Game over.

Under the terms of the Leather Apron Club term sheet, I and two other investors committed to invest a total of $450,000 subject to one condition. Because the results of the trial at Doon Government Hospital were so positive as to be suspicious, a second trial would have to show comparable results confirming the efficacy of DiaResQ.

The "comparable results" condition was more problematic than it appeared. Tim later confided in me that he'd seen it as a potentially insurmountable challenge at the time. The June 2010 trial had happened during the early monsoon season, amid elevated temperatures and humidity. By contrast, the follow-up trial would be performed in January, at a time when northern India experiences minimal rainfall and temperatures drop into the 30s Fahrenheit. Testing the product in an environment so dissimilar from the first trial invited the prospect of unexpected disease profiles and novel combinations of bacteria and viruses. The uncertainties associated with this seasonal variation kept Tim on edge.

In January 2011 Bimla returned to Dr. Joshi's clinic in Dehradun bearing packets of DiaResQ. Thirty-one pediatric patients with "serious" or "severe" diarrhea were treated with the PanTheryx product over a period of several days. The lifesaving treatment administered by Bimla and Dr. Joshi to five-month-old Rashni, recounted in the introduction, occurred during this trial. Despite any concerns Tim might have had, the trial results were essentially identical to the June 2010 results. All patients treated with the PanTheryx product displayed dramatic improvement within 24 hours.

Notified that the trial had yielded "substantially comparable trial results," the Leather Apron Club enthusiastically invested the remaining $277,000.

With the successful completion of the second trial, Dr. Joshi's mood shifted from skepticism to infatuation with Bimla and PanTheryx. Dr. Joshi happened to be the host of a popular television show in Dehradun, *Hello Doctor*. In the show, which covered important medical issues, audience members were encouraged to ask the host questions. Dr. Joshi pleaded with Bimla to appear as a guest on the show to discuss the PanTheryx product. Recognizing the importance of maintaining the company's low profile for the time being, Bimla politely declined.

During the next several weeks, the team in Boulder analyzed the data from the first two trials in order to optimize the product's formula. With the improved product and additional angel funding in the bank, Bimla returned to Dr. Joshi's clinic in late March to lead another, larger study. As she prepared to kick it off, the head of the hospital advised her that, contrary to the existing arrangement, PanTheryx would need to pay for the use of the clinic for this and any future trials. Suspecting the administrator of following an all-too-common local custom of allowing a process to move forward only if the appropriate officials are "rewarded," Bimla reacted with the tenacity emblematic of her Rajput warrior heritage. She rejected the request, packed her bags, and walked out the door.

Uncertain about where to turn, Bimla contacted one of the company's sales representatives at his office in Meerut to help identify local clinics that might host additional trials of the product. The employee suggested she join him there, while he began contacting doctors he knew from his sales network. With no direct air or bus service to Meerut and only irregular train departures, Bimla had no choice but to hail a taxi. The 110-mile trip from Dehradun, along a narrow, two-lane road out of the mountains through a dozen towns and villages, could take four hours. Getting there would be not only protracted and grueling, it could also be dangerous for a woman traveling alone.

The region encompassing Dehradun and Meerut, although heavily populated in parts, presented an unlikely menace: wild animals. Herds of wild elephants sometimes blocked roads or roamed through villages. Even in larger cities like Meerut, with a population of over a million, panthers, leopards, and tigers would occasionally terrorize citizens and even force the shutdown of schools and offices.

No elephants charged, but as Bimla's taxi descended the mountain road, her driver swerved to avoid an oncoming car and landed a glancing blow to the side of the other vehicle. Ignoring Bimla's demand to stop the car, the taxi driver continued on his way. As they approached the next village, they discovered that the road ahead was blocked by hundreds of irate local citizens who had been alerted by the aggrieved driver of the other car. Forcing the taxi to a stop, the mob pulled the driver from the vehicle and began to beat him with their fists.

Although Bimla's first reaction was panic, her Rajput side won out. Wading into the middle of the crowd, she demanded that the violence cease. Her family remained prominent in the area, and she threatened to call highly placed officials in the region to report what was happening. The crowd immediately withdrew. After a brief negotiation, followed by a payment of the equivalent of $50, Bimla and her battered driver resumed their journey.

In Meerut, Bimla met with the company's sales representative, who had identified three promising local clinics. As expected, in each case the doctors in charge wanted to know the formula of the product.

Again, in each case, Bimla assured the physician that the product was food-based and perfectly safe. To further minimize concerns, she suggested each trial start with only 10 patients. The combination of Bimla's gentle persuasion and reassuring phone conversations with Dr. Joshi did the job: all three clinics would host trials.

The Meerut trials offer an instructive contrast in the socio-economic status of the clinics involved as well as the economic stratification of Indian society in general. In a hospital and outpatient clinic on the outskirts of Meerut, pediatrician Dr. A. K. Kaushik treats over 100 patients a day, most from destitute families in rural areas where diarrhea was commonplace. Because these families can't afford to transport their children to the hospital for anything but the most life-threatening emergencies, most of the patients he does see are extremely ill, brought in as a last resort. As a result, according to Dr. Kaushik, "any quick intervention at this point is a life-saver."

When Bimla arrived, she found that conditions at the Kaushik clinic paralleled those at the Doon Government Hospital: crowded, noxious, and unbearably hot. Located at the end of a narrow, dingy side-street in a heavily Muslim area of Meerut, the clinic occupied a small structure with a garage door for an entrance situated next to a used tire and welding shop. Patients sat patiently in the hot sun on dusty tires awaiting their turn with the doctor. Bimla's only escape from the turmoil of the clinic was an occasional break sitting in her air-conditioned rental car with the engine running and the windows closed, sometimes accompanied by children most at risk of succumbing to the heat.

At the opposite extreme from the Doon and Kaushik clinics was the Tara Child Care Center in Meerut. Founded in 1995 by Dr. Anuj Rastogi, one of the most respected pediatricians in northern India, the center offers services including growth monitoring, developmental assessment, early intervention/neurodevelopmental follow-up, special education, and speech and music therapy for special needs children. This litany of preventive care and treatment services would bewilder the uneducated families visiting Dr. Kaushik's clinic from rural slums. Most of Dr. Rastogi's patients come from well-to-do families in the large cities whose treatment expectations would be more aligned with those of a middle-class family in the United States. Unlike the chaotic, crowded, and frequently unsanitary conditions in clinics that treated children from the slums, the Tara Child Care Center was clean, orderly, and cheerful. Despite the difference in clientele and conditions, however, a large percentage of Dr. Rastogi's pediatric patients also suffered from acute infectious diarrhea. In a developing society like India, unclean food and water are ubiquitous societal equalizers. Pediatric diarrhea is an equal opportunity affliction.

As the trial progressed, Dr. Rastogi reported that the PanTheryx product was effective, safe, and fast. Whereas a normal diarrhea patient in his practice showed improvement only after six to seven days, "with this food product the disease lasts only two to three days and the patients start showing a good response after a first dose."

Because Dr. Rastogi's clinic was a highly respected, leading-edge treatment facility, word of this remarkable new intervention spread quickly. While most small companies would welcome any free publicity, the prospect was anathema to Tim and Bimla. Tim constantly stressed to me the importance of confidentiality when working in India: "You can get anything done, and make everything work," he explained, "if you are smart enough to stay under the radar." The corollary to this was that the moment you were noticed, everyone who hopes to "get paid by keeping you from doing what you are doing will show up." The company's objective at this stage was to be "silent and invisible so we could learn everything we needed to know."

During a typically hectic afternoon at the Tara center, Bimla recognized the presence of reporters from the local newspapers, flashing their press badges as they infiltrated the clinic and asking questions about the new "miracle powder." Bimla told Dr. Rastogi that if he didn't deal with the press, she would leave. Reluctant to be excluded from the trial, Dr. Rastogi called the reporters into his office and told them they were not welcome in the clinic. The reporters left, and the crisis was averted.

Then, a few days later, Bimla noticed several well-dressed men, unaccompanied by children, wandering the halls of the clinic with no apparent mission other than to inquire about the new treatment for diarrhea. Asking the clinic staff, Bimla discovered they were sales representatives from pharmaceutical companies that did business in India, busy gathering intelligence for their employers. Bimla demanded that all adults without children be excluded from the clinic. One gentleman, identified by the staff as a pharmaceutical sales representative, attempted to circumvent the restrictions by posing as the father of a child suffering from severe diarrhea. Claiming his child was too sick to bring to the clinic, he begged to be given several packets of the powder to take home with him to treat the suffering infant. He too was evicted from the premises.

Over the next few months, the three clinics treated 140 children suffering from severe, in many cases life-threatening, diarrhea, achieving the same "miraculous" results as earlier trials. Once again, the pediatricians—who had been treating similar cases for decades— were astonished by the speed and efficacy of the results. One wrote: "I am extremely happy to be associated with this new, revolutionary product."

Although the official trials were only taking place in northern India, friends of the company were allowed sample packets too. In March 2011, five Colorado families, including my own, traveled to the Peruvian Andes to visit the ancient ruins at Machu Picchu. Tim Starzl provided me with a supply of DiaResQ; this was South

America, after all. Good thing he did too: on our way back to Cusco from the site, four members of our party—including me—contracted severe diarrhea.

Most debilitated, ironically, was our guide, a fit and seasoned traveler who had spent years visiting South America. He was unable to leave his hotel room. Early in the afternoon, I slid three packets of the PanTheryx powder under his hotel room door, two of which he immediately consumed. The rest of us took it as well, and within a few hours, even our guide was almost fully recovered. By the next morning, we were completely cured.

My experience in Peru shortly after investing in the company quickly extinguished any lingering reservations I might have had regarding the efficacy of DiaResQ. As the company progressed over the next several years, similar firsthand testimonials forged a body of anecdotal evidence persuading investors, corporate partners, and others of the product's extraordinary speed and effectiveness. It's one thing to see an array of statistics from a field trial. It's another to have someone you know look you in the eye and tell you about the time the product saved his vacation.

The "comparable results" trial condition having been satisfied, followed by Bimla's subsequent trials in Meerut confirming the favorable results, the company focused its efforts on raising money. Through the summer of 2011, we leveraged our personal networks toward expanding the membership of the Leather Apron Club. Despite further infusions of capital, however, the company's momentum began to slow perceptibly.

As the investors had known from the beginning, Tim and Tom were smart and committed, but neither had deep experience in the world of nutritional and natural food products. They also lacked expertise in international trade and corporate partnering. There was a skill gap, and it was having an impact. The investors and the board concluded that for PanTheryx to flourish and fulfill the vision of the founders, an orderly transition of leadership would be essential. The company needed people at the helm with the requisite experience.

Recruiting an experienced team for an underfunded and virtually anonymous company posed yet another challenge. Getting it done quickly would propel the company forward; a prolonged search would risk disarray and potential extinction.

6

Boulder

It's not about money; it's about doing something that makes people's lives better.
—Mo Siegel, co-founder and CEO, Celestial Seasonings

Successfully scaling an early-stage company entails a witches' brew of technical expertise, managerial skill, capital, and entrepreneurial culture. Had PanTheryx not managed to put down roots in Boulder, the company's path forward as a producer of food-based therapeutic and nutritional products might have been compromised. Instead, thanks in part to one of Boulder's earliest entrepreneurs, PanTheryx was able to use the city, with its entrepreneurial drive, early-stage capital, management expertise, medical technology, and established natural foods companies, as its launching pad.

Drivers motoring northwest 25 miles from Denver on Colorado Highway 36 gradually ascend a ridge overlooking a pristine valley.

Perforating the nearby foothills to the west, a phalanx of vertical sandstone slabs reaches skyward toward 14,000-foot mountain peaks tracing the continental divide. To the east, the Great Plains of the American Midwest stretch to the horizon, eventually transected by the Mississippi River, over 800 miles in the distance. In the center of the valley sits Boulder.

Viewed from the crest of the ridge, Boulder might be mistaken for a remote town in a sparsely populated state; a place where urban sprawl had never considered taking up residence. Within the town's compact environs, buildings only occasionally rise above a fourth story, each one looking out of place amid the cohesive clarity of the surrounding structures.

The town of Boulder was formed in 1859, the year of the first reported gold discovery in the mountains of Colorado, followed in 1876 by the admission of Colorado as the 38th state in the Union and, in 1877, the opening of the University of Colorado Boulder campus. During the 1960s, the town's population began to swell, accelerated by the arrival of a large IBM plant and an influx of technology companies and government research laboratories. Many cities enjoy an unexpected commercial boom, but Boulder's leaders displayed remarkable foresight in handling this one. To prevent the placid environment from being overrun by development, Boulder approved the nation's first tax specifically designed to preserve the open space surrounding the town. Deemed by its inhabitants to be vital to the town's livability, Boulder's open space eventually grew to nearly 100,000 acres, laced with over 300 miles of biking and hiking trails. Anticipating a potential water shortage in the west, the city even purchased its own glacier.

With its abundant sunshine, open space, accessible mountain recreation, and high-tech jobs, Boulder became home to a dynamic population of bikers and rock climbers, triathletes and trust funders, skiers and sailplane pilots, professors and politicians, and—to the benefit of the growing local economy—entrepreneurs. In *Startup Communities*, local entrepreneur and venture capitalist Brad Feld details Boulder's remarkable evolution from a sleepy college town into a hotbed of technological innovation, suggesting that Boulder may have the "highest entrepreneurial density in the world."

Attracted by Boulder's freewheeling entrepreneurial spirit, Tim Starzl chose the town to launch his first startup, BioStar, in the early 1980s. He went on to found a series of other companies there over the next 30 years. In the same years, homegrown venture capital firms emerged around Boulder and Denver, obviating the need for local entrepreneurs to take a ritual pilgrimage to Boston or San Francisco in search of capital.

By the time Tim started PanTheryx in 2007, Boulder had evolved into a perfect setting to nurture a food-based nutritional products company, boasting plenty of local industry and managerial expertise. The foundation for this platform had been forged almost 40 years earlier. In 1969, Mo Siegel, a 20-year-old college dropout, began concocting tea blends from herbs he and his future wife scavenged from the mountain valleys and hillsides near Boulder. Within a few years, Siegel and others founded an herbal tea company, Celestial Seasonings, one of the country's first natural food companies, whose success spawned a proliferation of local businesses focused on nutritional supplements and organic, natural, and medicinal foods. Boulder eventually became the "epicenter of the natural products industry."

By 1976, Celestial was the top-selling herbal tea brand in the United States and was beginning to expand overseas. As his company gained momentum, Siegel started seeking out experienced executives to bolster his management team.

While attending a trade show in Boston in 1978, Siegel met a tall, engaging Canadian named Keith Brenner. After an early stint with

General Foods following college, Brenner had joined Pepsi in Canada, moving on to run five plant operations in the Philippines before being named vice president of marketing for Africa. At this point, Brenner left behind a promising career at Pepsi to start a fruit nectar company on Maui in Hawaii. This unique background—international executive for two leading food and beverage companies and then founder of a natural food company—caught Siegel's attention. A consummate salesman, Siegel invited Brenner to visit Boulder, where he promptly convinced him to sell his nectar company to Celestial and become its vice president of marketing. Over the next six years, Celestial grew to over $40 million in sales and, in 1984, was acquired by Kraft Foods.

After leaving Celestial in 1985, Brenner remained in Boulder, working as a strategic planning consultant. One of his clients, OmegaTech, was an early-stage nutritional food company. Brenner helped them recruit a new president and CEO, Mark Braman. Brenner and Braman would each go on to play a pivotal role in the PanTheryx story.

Mark Braman was the second of seven children in a blue-collar family in Midland, located in the Saginaw Valley of central Michigan. His father worked as an electrician while his mom managed the household, doing her best to coordinate the schedules of a house full of fanatical athletes. Midland, world headquarters of Dow Chemical Company, was a company town of 35,000 where, Mark later recalled, "most of the people either worked for Dow or for a company that provided products or services to Dow."

Like many a small town in the Midwest, Midland was engulfed by frenzied enthusiasm for high school football every autumn. Midland High School's team, aptly named the Chemics, was a perennial powerhouse, competing in a packed 10,000-seat stadium. On Friday nights, it assumed the trappings of a revival meeting, with inspirational pep talks, chants, and cheers.

Although he and his siblings played every sport available in a small midwestern town, by his senior year at Midland, Braman had focused on track and field and football. With a muscular six-foot-plus frame, Mark was a star running back and defensive back on the football team and a state high-jump champion. In his junior year, university football coaches began calling on the Braman household, hoping to recruit young Mark to join their programs. He was drawn to the University of Michigan, where Bo Schembechler was in the middle of his legendary 21-year reign as one of the most successful coaches in the history of college football.

During Braman's time playing for the Michigan Wolverines in the late 1970s, Schembechler amassed several of his most memorable seasons, winning three Big Ten Championships and appearing in three Rose Bowls and one Orange Bowl. Braman was a stand-out in the defensive backfield, starting 24 straight games during his junior and senior years, being named to the Big Ten All-Academic Team in 1979, and playing for the East All-Star Team in the 1980 Japan Bowl.

Years later, as a successful business executive and entrepreneur, Braman told me Schembechler was one of the few people other than his own father who had profoundly influenced his life. "A lot of the reasons why I'm doing what I'm doing today," he said, "are because of the life lessons I learned from Bo."

Braman also had the distinction of playing in a game that will go down in Wolverine history. In the 1979 Rose Bowl, Michigan played the University of Southern California in a game many predicted would determine the number-one ranking in college football that year. In the second quarter, USC All-American Charles White fumbled the ball as he dove into the end zone from the three-yard line. Michigan recovered the fumble on the one-yard line, and photographs later confirmed that the ball clearly never reached the goal line. The line judge, who was behind Braman and therefore could not see the ball, ruled it a touchdown, causing Michigan to lose the game. Shortly thereafter, USC was named the number-one team in the country by the college coaches poll.

The infamous "phantom touchdown" has since resided on virtually every list of the worst calls in the history of college football and, in at least one case, "the worst call in the history of sports." (This would not be the last time Mark Braman experienced first-hand the capricious nature of unfettered officialdom.)

After trying out for three professional football teams, Braman decided on the business world, getting an entry-level position in his hometown with Dow Chemical. Shortly thereafter, he married Jennie Bath, who had also attended both Midland High School and the University of Michigan, where she had been an All-American cheerleader. Upon completing the Dow executive training program, Mark was offered a position in Denver with Dow's fast-growing "enhanced oil recovery" division, selling specialty chemicals to large oil companies. Mark readily accepted and moved west, eventually settling near Boulder.

In 1984, Braman's growing acclaim as a sales executive caught Pfizer's eye. Pfizer's chemical division, having identified the oil industry as an expansion opportunity, approached Braman to join what amounted to a startup within Pfizer to pursue enhanced oil recovery. At 25, Mark made the first of many high-risk decisions that would propel his business career, vaulting from a secure trajectory with an established company to an embryonic venture with indeterminate prospects. When Mark told his mother about his decision to work for the pharmaceutical giant, she responded, "Who's Pfizer?"

"It was my first taste of anything entrepreneurial," Mark recalled. "A new business built from scratch."

By the late 1980s Braman had worldwide responsibility for the Pfizer Oil Field Products Division, negotiating and building international alliances, launching new products, licensing technologies to broaden the product portfolio, and negotiating supply and service agreements in places including China. In the early 1990s, Pfizer decided to sell the oil products division and moved Braman to its headquarters in New York City, where he made an auspicious career move into life sciences, joining the company's Nutrition Group.

During that decade, Pfizer enjoyed rapid growth driven by a robust pipeline of new products. In 1997 and 1998 *Fortune* named Pfizer "the world's most admired pharmaceutical company." By the end of the decade, it would be the largest pharmaceutical company in the world. Working in the company's New York headquarters during this period and assuming increasingly significant leadership positions in business development for its growing nutraceuticals business was, in Braman's opinion, "exactly the place to be."

This experience exposed Mark to a new world of entrepreneurial ventures and fast-growing startup companies. Pfizer's massive cash flow combined with its desire to dramatically expand its product portfolio made it possible for him to lead a series of investments in small companies with cutting-edge technologies. He was involved in licensing new products, assisting in formulating startups' strategic plans, and even helping them to become public companies. Before long, Mark began to contemplate the idea of running his own small company where he could "build the culture, hire the team, and grow an enterprise into something substantial."

Despite the perquisites of chauffeur-driven cars, corporate aircraft, a lofty compensation package, and the spacious offices associated with being a senior executive at Pfizer, Braman sensed something was missing. By the late 1990s, Mark and Jennie had five children immersed in school events and team sports, while Mark was commuting from suburban Connecticut to Manhattan and traveling the world on business. When the opportunity arose in 1997 to become

CEO of OmegaTech and move the family back to Colorado, he decided the time was right and "took the plunge."

In hindsight, Mark's decision to shift his career from a *Fortune* 500 company to the capricious realm of entrepreneurship was hardly surprising. If you were to ask a football coach to name the traits most valued in a defensive back, he would likely mention competitiveness, resourcefulness, adaptability, determination, focus, and relentless pursuit. He would also require characteristics like leadership, teamwork, and an indomitable work ethic. Pose the same question to a venture capitalist or board of directors seeking a chief executive for an early-stage company, and the response will be virtually identical. In Mark Braman, the coach and the venture capitalist would see the perfect candidate.

In the summer of 1997, the seven members of the Braman family flew into Denver International Airport and drove to Boulder, where Mark would assume his new duties as CEO. Before they reached their hotel, one of the children asked if they could stop in and see the new office. Mark obliged. Walking into the OmegaTech world headquarters was "an eye-opener." The company had six employees and only enough cash to operate for about two months. The entire research laboratory would have fit comfortably into Mark's former office at Pfizer. His new office, which he shared with two other employees, was less than half the size of the research laboratory.

When the family returned to the car, Jennie turned to Mark and asked: "What have you done?" Always the optimist, Mark responded, "Don't worry. We'll be okay. This is going to work."

7

The New Team

The ones who are crazy enough to think they can change
the world, are the ones who do.

—Steve Jobs

Mark Braman was the seventh employee to join OmegaTech, a
pioneer in the production of omega-3 fatty acids, or DHA, for use
in infant formula, supplements, functional and medicinal foods, as
well as, in a purified form, lipid management drugs. Omega-3 fatty
acids were typically extracted from oily, cold-water fish like salmon,
sardines, cod, and trout. OmegaTech, on the other hand, produced
its DHA products using a patented algae fermentation technology,
yielding a superior product.

The OmegaTech narrative in many ways parallels Braman's subsequent experience at PanTheryx. At the time, it was known that the
DHA contained in mother's milk provided a crucial nutrient for brain

and eye development in infants. OmegaTech's product allowed DHA to be cost-effectively added to baby formula for the first time, extending the benefits of breastfeeding, not unlike the role of DiaResQ in effectively loaning the benefits of the mother's immune system to the child.

During Mark's tenure as CEO of OmegaTech from 1997 to 2002, the company grew from a cash-starved early-stage enterprise to a leading player in the functional food and nutritional supplements industry. While raising over $40 million in venture capital funding, the company swelled from 7 to 75 employees and increased its portfolio from 10 to over 100 patents either issued or pending.

Transforming an early-stage company into a prosperous enterprise requires more than a skillful leader; it demands a diverse, talented, and cohesive team with industry experience and expertise. It helps if many of the individuals on the team have worked together in prior endeavors. For OmegaTech, Mark tapped his personal network of relationships, reaching back into the pool of talent at Pfizer to recruit a cadre of trusted former associates, a team that would ultimately follow him into his next three entrepreneurial ventures.

Rob Driver grew up in the small college town of Hillsdale, Michigan, less than 150 miles south of Mark Braman's hometown of Midland. His father owned the local shoe store; his mother occasionally helped out there. Rob had an informal understanding with his father requiring that he, too, would work at the store unless he could find a better paying summer job. He unfailingly did.

After receiving a degree in chemistry and biology from Central Michigan University, Rob went to the University of Kentucky for his master's. While in graduate school, presaging his future roles at OmegaTech and PanTheryx, he worked on Department of Agriculture and Engineering assignments at local poultry farms. Rob went on to a career as an industrial microbiologist in fermentation-based manufacturing. Joining Pfizer in 1985, he was eventually moved to the New York City headquarters, where he began working with Mark Braman in the Nutrition Group.

Food dominated family discourse when George Stagnitti was growing up, in a small town in northern New Jersey near the New York border. George's father was a food broker, who acted as an intermediary between manufacturers and distributors or retailers, including high-end restaurants.

"Dad was always bringing home new food products for us to evaluate and discuss over dinner," George recalls. Growing up, George was fascinated with science and technology, as well as food, leading him to secure a degree in food and nutrition at the University of Maryland at College Park, one of the few institutions in the country offering such a program. Most days he also worked at the university dairy, milking the cows at six each morning before going to class. After securing a master's in chemistry, Stagnitti earned a Management of Technology degree from Rensselaer Polytechnic Institute in upstate New York, America's oldest technological research university. It was at Rensselaer that he learned the importance of integrating technology and business, or how technology could be used to improve consumer products and make them more successful in the marketplace.

George started his career in the mid-1980s in the flavor industry, where he came to champion an enduring truth in the world of food and nutrition: to succeed, a product must meet the consumer's expectations for flavor and texture. No exceptions.

In the early 1990s, Stagnitti joined Pfizer in Groton, Connecticut, where he led a group commercializing food, flavor, and sensory science technologies for the company's nutritional and functional food program. Before long, he became acquainted with Rob Driver and Mark Braman, eventually partnering with Mark in seeking out new business opportunities for Pfizer. One of the businesses they studied closely was OmegaTech.

Soon after he took over as OmegaTech's CEO, Mark convinced Rob to join the company as vice president of manufacturing. By 2000, George had been convinced to join the team as director of product applications. By that point, he was ready to transition from "the bureaucratic, slower-moving culture of a large company to an entrepreneurial environment." With his love of technological innovation, it's no surprise George would jump at the chance, however risky, to "have a greater impact in moving products forward at an accelerated pace." OmegaTech would be the first of three early-stage Colorado companies in which Mark, Rob, and George would be pivotal in building a successful enterprise.

As the market for DHA-fortified food and beverage products grew, the OmegaTech team decided a merger with its largest competitor, publicly traded Martek Biosciences, would produce the most value for shareholders. After the deal closed in 2002, the team dispersed for a few years. Then Mark was asked by a venture capital group to become CEO of Efficas, Inc., a new Boulder startup. Efficas was more concept than company when Mark agreed to step in.

"Its only asset was a single computer," he recalled. "It had no products and no substantive business plan." Mark invited George to join him in developing a market and product strategy for the fledgling enterprise. They eventually formulated a mission: "to be a leader in bioactive solutions that measurably improve the quality of life of people with immune diseases." The focus would be on the development of nutritional products for managing the immune system of both humans and their pets.

In 2005, Rob had joined the company as vice president of manufacturing and the team was reunited. Once on board, Mark hired Julie Lindemann as Efficas' director of safety, regulatory, and clinical affairs. Julie had earned her PhD in plant pathology, with a minor in bacteriology, at the University of Wisconsin, and spent 25 years researching and commercializing new biotechnology and food products. The go-forward team was now complete.

With the onset of the recession in late 2007, unemployment nationally soared to 10 percent, financial institutions were declaring bankruptcy, and the availability of capital all but dried up. By March 2009, the Dow Jones Industrial Average had dropped more than 50 percent, venture capital firms were hoarding cash, and corporations were sidestepping relationships with smaller firms.

Efficas launched a medical food product, branded Efficas Care, which proved remarkably effective in reducing inflammation in the lungs and nasal passages of asthmatics. Despite this, the harsh investment climate following the start of the recession in 2007 took its toll. The investors could not agree on a financing strategy to sustain further growth and, in 2010, the company was sold to the owners of Hidden Villa Ranch, one of the largest egg producers in the country (and a future supplier to PanTheryx).

Back to Keith Brenner, former Celestial Seasonings marketing chief. After Tim and Bimla Starzl launched PanTheryx in 2007, the company's lawyer, Dave Cook, suggested that they meet with Keith, now a consultant, for help with strategic planning. Keith had a daughter-in-law of Indian descent and thought the PanTheryx connection might offer an opportunity to learn more about the country and its culture. After the meeting, he agreed to make a small investment and help out with sales and marketing from time to time. According to Brenner, he assumed the company would "never amount to anything big."

As he had done with OmegaTech, Brenner worked with PanTheryx on strategic marketing, including issues ranging from the size of the potential market to the most appealing packaging for the product.

At the board's request, he also canvassed his extensive personal network in the Boulder natural foods community for candidates who might be available to join the company as president and chief executive officer. In August 2011, Brenner discussed the company with Mark Braman. The timing was propitious, as Braman was wrapping up the sale of Efficas. Braman's résumé, tracing his path from large pharmaceutical company executive to nutritional food company entrepreneur, made him a perfect match for PanTheryx.

Beginning in early September 2011, a series of meetings was held between Mark and the PanTheryx team: Tim and Bimla, Keith Brenner, Diane Dustin (the company's office manager and all-around utility infielder), and members of the board. As the meetings progressed, Mark wrote Keith: "The more I look at this, the more interested/excited I get about the opportunity."

Everyone assumed that Tim would express the deepest skepticism, but he responded to the meetings with enthusiasm. "Mark understood in depth virtually everything we were talking about," he explained. Mark Braman was named president and CEO of PanTheryx on October 3. He also was elected to the board of directors.

Meanwhile, following the sale of Efficas, Rob Driver was savoring his uncluttered calendar, dabbling in consulting engagements, and "playing a fair bit of golf." One balmy October morning, he was warming up on the driving range when Keith Brenner happened by. Brenner chatted enthusiastically about the work he was doing at PanTheryx and told Rob to expect a call from Mark. In early November, Rob joined the team at PanTheryx as vice president, operations and manufacturing.

Seeing that Mark was intent upon reconvening the Pfizer/OmegaTech/Efficas team, Rob sensed that PanTheryx, like the prior ventures, would be "fun, unique, interesting, and challenging." Based on their earlier collaborations, he also had a "sense of how the organization would mesh." Expressing a sentiment that would be echoed many times by PanTheryx employees as the company grew, Rob said he was excited by "an opportunity to do some societal good," which he considered particularly important at that point in his career.

Julie Lindemann, another important member of the team at Efficas, also signed on around this time, taking the role of vice president of safety, regulatory, and clinical affairs. A calm, steady woman, Julie's soothing voice and tranquil but authoritative demeanor put people in mind of their favorite high school teacher. With years of clinical trials and regulatory clearance work ahead, Mark's recruitment of Julie represented a vital addition.

Mark's final move in assembling the PanTheryx management team was to bring one last OmegaTech alum on board: George Stagnitti, its former product applications director. Stagnitti, however, had a competing offer he felt he couldn't refuse. In January 2012, he joined Synthetic Genomics, Inc., a company founded by scientist Craig Venter. Venter, widely known for his work in genomic research, had led the first team to sequence the human genome. As vice president for nutritional products at Synthetic Genomics, George would lead the company's product and commercial development efforts in the food and nutritional products program. As George described it, Venter wanted to "genetically manipulate single-cell organisms to create next-generation protein products." By synthesizing new food products in a test tube, Venter hoped to "help feed a growing world population," according to Stagnitti. "They had the technology," George explained. "The challenge was, how do you make it commercially viable?" Again, Stagnitti was pivoting to a fresh career challenge, another attempt to "integrate the business and technology pieces" in a new generation of products.

Although disappointed with Stagnitti's decision, Mark could only plunge into the daunting web of issues facing PanTheryx. He felt optimistic, however, that by successfully steering the company forward, he might eventually convince his former colleague to reconsider.

With a new team on board, Mark scrambled to gain a deeper understanding of the PanTheryx technology, market, intellectual property position, and regulatory landscape. Most urgently, he went to work ensuring the company didn't run out of money. Shortly after joining the company in October, Braman had determined there was cash on hand to keep the doors open until the end of January. He immediately turned to members of the Leather Apron Club as well as several potential investors who had held off on making a commitment until the new management team was in place. His message now underscored the industry experience of the new team, the imminent filing of the final patent, and the remarkable effectiveness of the product in the open-label field trials in India.

In an early meeting, a skeptical investor challenged Mark to name any comparable product that had come out of nowhere to solve a baffling medical enigma so quickly and effectively. Thinking back to the product pipeline from his Pfizer days, Mark's spontaneous response was humorous but accurate: "Viagra!" This answer would come in handy with many skeptics to come.

On November 22, 2011, PanTheryx filed United States Patent Application Number US 2012/0141458 A1 with the United States Patent Office. The patent, "Composition and Methods for Treatment in Broad-Spectrum Undifferentiated or Mixed Clinical Applications," named the inventor as Timothy W. Starzl of Boulder, Colorado.

By the following January, Mark and the team had raised an additional $700,000, bringing the Leather Apron Club angel round to a close. The club, now made up of 12 individuals and families, had invested a total of $1.6 million in PanTheryx since December 2010. Among the members of this select group was Mo Siegel, the founder of Celestial Seasonings and the father of the natural foods industry in Boulder.

The PanTheryx team went to work drafting a fresh business plan presentation, proposing a new investment round totaling $4 million at a price of $2 per share. Validating the new management team, the per share price represented a 40 percent increase over the price paid by members of the Leather Apron Club in the earlier round, valuing the company at $9 million before the infusion of any new capital.

After reviewing the final patent application, the team concluded that, rather than offering a single product or solution, the company's intellectual property represented a potential platform for dozens of food-based therapeutic products. This interpretation prompted a subtle but important change in the fundraising presentation. Rather than confining the company's market to the pediatric diarrhea market, the investor presentation embraced a more expansive profile as a medical nutrition company, emphasizing PanTheryx's "broad-based medical nutrition technology platform with a compelling intellectual property position."

***

Adhering to the strategy developed by Tim, Bimla, and Keith Brenner the prior year, the new team continued to focus on India as the ideal country to launch the product. Indian headquarters would be consolidated in Meerut, with 8 to 10 employees by mid-2012. The plan called for finished packaged goods to be ready for shipment to India by April, forecasting $15 million to $20 million in revenue in the first year of market rollout in India.

Mark later told me that, even as the company proceeded with plans for an India launch, he was haunted by concerns that results of the earlier trials in India were "too good to be true." To allay his apprehension, he proposed that Julie, whom he had known for many years and trusted implicitly, accompany Bimla to India to conduct the largest trial to date.

Mark arranged a trip to India in January, joined by Tim, Bimla, and Keith, to meet with employees, lawyers, headhunters, public relations firms, and doctors. Julie would follow to join Bimla for the latest field trial using material from new egg sources.

Whereas each of the earlier trials had involved about 60 children, the new plan called for 100. Rather than return to the smaller clinics where the last trials had been held, Bimla identified one in Meerut whose lead doctor was willing to run a trial with that many patients in a week.

As their work on the additional trial began, Meerut's late February temperatures were in the mid-70s, balmy compared to the sweltering summer months. After meeting with the new doctor, the PanTheryx contingent began training a dozen staff members to work on the trial in a series of grueling sessions running until 10 o'clock every evening.

Before Mark returned home, he spoke privately with Julie. Ignoring the twelve-and-a-half hour time difference between Meerut and Boulder, he told her to call him immediately, regardless of the time of day, as soon as she saw any evidence the product was working.

Unfortunately, after the prep work was complete and the trial was about to begin, the clinic's doctor demanded to know the contents of DiaResQ. When Bimla refused to divulge it, the doctor, in Bimla's words, "panicked," hastily arranging a visit with the district's chief medical officer. Bimla received word that a team of officials was on its way to confiscate the PanTheryx product. With no time to lose, Bimla and Julie packed up and departed immediately.

Returning to the clinics operated by Dr. Kaushik and Dr. Rastogi—who labeled the episode at the previous clinic "a lot of nonsense"—a smaller trial was hurriedly devised involving up to 30 children. On February 25, the first three patients were enrolled. Julie, seeing the product administered for the first time, was startled by the frailty and morbidity of the young patients.

At the end of the first day, she emailed an update to the rest of the team: "The product was very willingly consumed by the patients— they seemed to enjoy it a lot. Even kids who could not keep water down and were refusing other food took the product readily and exhibited no negative after-effects. There seems to be something almost immediately soothing about the product."

On the following day, as soon as Julie completed her observation of the first three children who had taken DiaResQ, she called Mark in Boulder, where it was three o'clock in the morning. Already half-awake in anticipation of a call, Mark answered immediately to hear her report. "You're not going to believe this," she said, "but all three children are normal." A relieved Mark shared the news with his wife and went back to sleep. As requested, Julie called Mark each night of the trial about the same time.

Later the same day, Julie emailed her report to the rest of the team: "All three of the patients returned for their second day and all three had improved dramatically. Parents reported that diarrhea had stopped and stools were normal or absent. Bottom line: the material is performing as expected so far." This pattern continued for the next week, all patients returning the second day exhibiting "no diarrhea or vomiting and improved well-being, alertness, and activity with no side effects." The results were so compelling that Julie and Bimla decided to close enrollment at 16. Belying her usual circumspection, Julie jubilantly emailed the rest of the team back in Boulder: "We have a winner!"

The PanTheryx product launch plan for India had been thoughtfully formulated over several months: hire several hundred direct sales representatives concentrated in a few highly populated metropolitan areas, thereby proving the sales potential and customer demand for the product. The Meerut area alone offered a viable market, with over eight million inhabitants and sprawling slums where diarrhea was endemic. Growing sales momentum in a handful of cities would, in turn, give the company considerable leverage to negotiate favorable agreements with large pharmaceutical companies and distributors to partner in rolling the product out nationwide. Another factor favoring a direct sales force, according to local experts engaged by the company, was that any local distributor would probably attempt to steal the technology and develop knock-off products while PanTheryx was in startup mode and relatively defenseless.

As the rest of the team wrapped up their meetings in India and departed for home, Keith Brenner, in his role as vice president of marketing, visited with local doctors and hospitals alongside the company's sales representatives. Having spent many hours developing a marketing plan and financial projections, Brenner wanted firsthand experience of conditions in the local hospitals. He wanted to see how medical products were currently distributed and to hear about the pediatric diarrhea problem directly from caregivers.

These meetings were highly encouraging. After a cordial visit at one hospital, a doctor invited Brenner to his house to meet his family and join them in attending a party that evening. Brenner discovered that most professionals he met in Meerut were delighted to connect with American businesspeople. This made it possible for a savvy networker "to open pretty much any door you want."

Although he garnered worthwhile market data canvassing health providers in Meerut, Brenner also unearthed market dynamics that were cause for concern. After hearing about the product, several doctors told the team to return in three days, and then stop by every three days or so after that. Noting Brenner's bewildered reaction to this odd response, the sales reps revealed the tacit message: these doctors were expecting a present of some kind to be delivered at each visit. Once they were satisfied with what they'd been given, they would give the product a try. Over time, the company found this practice to be pervasive. In response, the management adopted a firm and consistent response: not interested.

Another concern: India's health-care system includes a large number of unaccredited, unqualified, and, all too often, life-threatening health-care providers colloquially known as "quacks." The problem is so pervasive that Delhi's Medical Council has an "anti-quackery committee." The state government has debated introducing an "Anti-Quackery Bill." In rural areas, "quacks" outnumbered qualified doctors 23 to 1. Because the Indian population is overwhelmingly poor, most families turn to qualified physicians and clinics only as a last resort. Quacks, who habitually overprescribe expensive antibiotics and off-label therapeutics, enjoy a flourishing livelihood.

Mindful of the outsized number of quacks treating the clientele PanTheryx was determined to reach, Brenner did not hesitate to call on quacks as he researched the market. During a visit with a prototypical quack in Meerut, the provider argued quite passionately that everything he did was "above board," emphasizing that his sole objective was to "save lives and serve the community." After the encounter, Brenner asked the sales reps how much of what they had just heard was true. The reps quickly responded: "Not even one percent."

***

By late summer of 2012, George Stagnitti began to realize that "the large consumer products companies were not ready to embrace Craig Venter's vision." Stubborn market resistance to genetically modified food and nutrition products stymied Synthetic Genomics' near-term commercial viability. Despite his respect for Venter and his work, George was growing impatient "waiting for the market to catch up" with the company's products. In the meantime, Mark affably persisted in trying to recruit George. George conceded the opportunity was becoming "very compelling."

Having worked with Julie and Rob in the past, George took their enthusiasm for the PanTheryx product seriously. He also concluded that Julie's feedback from the latest pilot study in India was "remarkable." So, in late August, he finally agreed to join the company, as executive vice president. His decision was based on some key attributes of the business: "the global need, the demonstrated effectiveness, the reasonably simple and accepted composition, and the right cost structure."

While Mark focused on raising a new round of financing, Rob Driver moved to quickly establish relationships with suppliers of raw materials and contract manufacturers. An egg supply relationship was negotiated with Hidden Villa Ranch in Fullerton, California, one of the nation's largest egg producers and distributors. Hidden Villa had been founded in the 1940s as a family chicken ranch and egg-delivery business. Under Tim Luberski, the son of the original founder, Hidden Villa had become one of the country's fastest-growing private companies by the 1980s. In another example of the entrepreneurial value of personal networks, Tim was no stranger to Mark Braman. Hidden Villa had been the original egg supplier to OmegaTech, Mark's first startup when he had moved to Colorado. More importantly, Mark had served on the board of Hidden Villa since 2003.

PanTheryx also began negotiations with the world's largest supplier of high-quality colostrum products, Phoenix-based APS BioGroup. Upon returning from a two-day meeting with the APS management team, Mark was effusive about the quality of the team and the operation, at one point proclaiming "I think we should acquire this company." At the time, the notion of PanTheryx, with no revenue and just enough cash to stay in operation for a couple of months, acquiring a successful and profitable company like APS struck me as either profoundly audacious or simply delusional. As we would learn, Mark was entirely serious; he was already charting his long-term strategic vision for PanTheryx.

Although most of the original members of the Leather Apron Club agreed to participate in the new round of funding, additional investor prospects would have to be identified to round up $4 million. The earlier investors reached into their various networks of business associates and acquaintances, generating a steady stream of contacts for Mark to pursue. The growing list included individuals who were rumored to have access to substantial wealth. Impressed with the quality, transparency, and loyalty of the Leather Apron Club members, Mark insisted any new investors be vetted closely, with reference checks and extensive face-to-face meetings. As we shortly learned, his caution was warranted.

In early 2012, a Denver investor suggested Mark contact Kimberly Fontenot, a woman in the Houston area purported to have access to a large group of very wealthy angel investors. Returning from a business trip to Mexico in May, Mark stopped in Houston to meet with her. In her early 50s, she struck Mark as sincere, confident, and credible. After Mark briefed her on the PanTheryx investment opportunity, Fontenot gushed with enthusiasm, calling it "the most compelling opportunity I have ever seen." Mark tactfully inquired about her contacts and what process he might expect should they proceed with a business relationship. Her response left him stunned.

Fontenot told Mark that, during a 1990 trip to the Middle East, she had been captured by terrorists and held captive for several months. Ultimately, she was rescued by a secretive group that paid her ransom, making the exchange for her in a remote desert locale. After being shepherded back to the United States, she learned that her liberator was a cabal of billionaires known only as "the Patriot

Group." According to Fontenot, the group worked behind the scenes to arrange the release of Americans captured in foreign countries. Fontenot, now a friend and trusted advisor of the group, would share investment opportunities with them on behalf of early-stage companies for an upfront fee of $5,000.

Fontenot supplied PanTheryx with the names of 10 investors, prominent members of the *Forbes* or *Bloomberg* lists of billionaires. Information was exchanged directly between the company and the investors by email or in phone conversations arranged by Fontenot. A typical investor email began: "My name is Boone"—Pickens, of course—"and Kimberly is a lovely friend of ours. She recommends your company highly…"

Discussions by phone were surprisingly superficial and brief. As Mark and dozens of other eager entrepreneurs would eventually learn, Ms. Fontenot's narrative was an elaborate hoax. In contrast to many other businesses, however, PanTheryx spent only minimal time and effort pursuing this avenue. Another misstep avoided. In April 2013, FBI agents raided Fontenot's home. She was charged with "executing a fraudulent investment scheme" involving the use of fake email accounts in the names of wealthy investors and voice actors hired to impersonate investors during conference calls with the "victim business owners." Seven months later, Fontenot pleaded guilty and was convicted of wire fraud in a Texas federal court. She was sentenced to three years in prison and ordered to repay more than $115,000 in fees.

Approaching the end of his first full year as CEO of PanTheryx, Mark focused on one more hire to round out the management team: an in-house lawyer to coordinate the plethora of legal issues facing the company. He once again turned to the support network that had proved so reliable in his earlier startups.

Scott Hyman grew up 10 miles north of the George Washington

Bridge on the New Jersey side of the Hudson River, less than a dozen miles from George Stagnitti's childhood home. Scott's father, Micky, pursued an eclectic career ranging from selling nuclear power plants in Europe and the Middle East for General Electric to serving as general counsel of CBS Records and president of the Home Video division of MGM/UA Home Entertainment Group. By the time Scott graduated from Villanova Law School in 1991, Micky was a prominent intellectual property and entertainment lawyer in New York City. Scott joined the practice.

Although the firm had many high-profile clients, its claim to fame, according to Scott, was that it managed entertainment licensing for the Teenage Mutant Ninja Turtles franchise, the first billion-dollar franchise marketed specifically for children. The firm handled the licensing of live shows, music, television, and hit movies for the franchise, including the first Teenage Mutant Ninja Turtles film, which became the highest-grossing independent film ever released up to that time.

In 1994, to the dismay of his father, Scott left the firm to pursue various entrepreneurial and operational opportunities. By 1997, ready to settle down, he asked himself: "If I could live anywhere in the world, where would I go?" The answer, he realized, was Boulder, Colorado. His operational roles allowed Scott to gain invaluable management experience. He recalls the steep learning curve as he "learned how to make stuff" and "made every possible mistake you could make importing a product from China."

Ultimately, Scott set up a law practice serving as outside general counsel to several companies in the Boulder area, calling it "the greatest law gig you could possibly have." Mark Braman began to engage Scott for various projects, and the two developed a strong working relationship. In contrast to Mark's folksy, soft-spoken midwestern charm, Scott was a hard-nosed lawyer whose sometimes gruff personality and New Jersey accent belied a pragmatic, resolute, and highly professional practitioner.

In December 2012, Mark began selling Scott on PanTheryx as a "tremendous opportunity," inviting him to join the company as in-house general counsel. Although convinced that the opportunity to hold employee stock options offered potential financial rewards, Scott was even more captivated by the company's mission: "I was keenly aware of the potential impact the product would have in the lives of the people we were helping." In the end, he said, he "couldn't pass it up."

8

India Impasse

No people whose word for "yesterday" is the same as their word for "tomorrow" can be said to have a firm grip on the time.

—Salman Rushdie, *Midnight's Children*

The Starzls' initial vision of PanTheryx focused on the strategic importance of one crucial market, one population of children, one familiar, yet challenging, culture: India.

As Tim often reminds me, he targeted pediatric diarrhea because "children die from it; most adults don't." The alarming statistics from India confirmed this conclusion. India has the world's largest population of children under the age of five. Collectively, these children endure over 380 million episodes of diarrhea each year. In 2011, the year PanTheryx filed its final patent application, UNICEF estimated that more children under the age of five had died in India that year than in any other county. The number of childhood deaths in India each year exceeds 1.7 million, of which more than 400,000 are caused by diarrhea, second only to Afghanistan on a per capita basis. The UNICEF report highlights India as a country where "rapid economic growth and strong inflows of trade and investment in recent years have failed to bring about corresponding reduction of inequities in under-five mortality."

Although the altruistic goal of reducing the appalling child death rate provided a compelling narrative for the creation of PanTheryx, the size of the market opportunity—assuming the product could be sold at an acceptable price—represented an enormous business opportunity as well. Most medical treatments sold in India are classified as generics, which don't require a doctor's prescription. The Indian market for so-called nutraceuticals, including dietary supplements and functional foods, has been estimated at $1.5 billion, a share of which PanTheryx hoped to capture with its product.

Another factor driving the company's focus on India was the founders' comprehensive understanding of the culture, traditions, and business climate there. Bimla had been born and raised in a prominent business family in northern India, and Tim and Bimla had made numerous subsequent trips there over the years. The Starzls knew the Indian market better than most Americans in the industry. This was a strategic advantage.

The company's October 2010 business summary boldly forecasted launching the product in India in the second half of 2011. This document, citing the company's sales of generic drugs by its in-house sales force over the previous three years, noted its familiarity with Indian distribution networks and its extensive business relationships in the country.

Notwithstanding the company's early optimism, a baffling range of obstacles confronts any foreign company doing business in India. Particularly daunting for a small, early-stage one like PanTheryx are the pervasive corruption, the bureaucracy, and the unpredictable regulatory environment. The prestigious Singapore-based Political and Economic Risk Consultancy issued a report in January 2012 naming India as the country with the worst bureaucracy in Asia, citing inadequate infrastructure, corruption, and lack of accountability for erroneous decisions.

These obstacles, as well as many other attributes of systemic dysfunction in India, are addressed in *An Uncertain Glory: India and Its Contradictions*, co-authored by Nobel Prize–winning economist Amartya Sen. The authors write: "Corruption has become such an endemic feature of Indian administration and commercial life that in some parts of the country nothing moves in the intended direction unless the palm of the deliverer is greased."

Underscoring the "comprehensive neglect of accountability" among government employees in the country's sprawling bureaucracy, the authors note its corrosive effect on transparency, honesty, and reliable decision-making. The result is a toxic culture enabled by government officials possessing "sole command—or oligarchic dominance—over giving licenses" without countervailing opportunities for review or appeal of tainted decisions. In short, doing business in India is not for the faint of heart.

Through 2010 and most of 2011, the Starzls prodded the company forward with modest angel funding, relying on the creation of close working relationships with Indian officials and medical clinics, many secured through family and business connections, with little concern for regulatory minefields. Their guiding strategy rested on getting "inside the system," gaining an understanding of the inner workings of programs and departments, ingratiating themselves with decision makers, and eventually applying pressure to achieve their objectives.

Bimla was singularly effective in identifying a path to the "inside" and building the necessary relationships. When I asked Tim how

Bimla did this, he responded affectionately: from what he could tell, the Indians saw her as "a very nice Rajput lady who was generous and gracious in a traditional vein and kindly to everyone." Tim adds that, in his opinion, "the true, functional India is for Indians, not foreigners."

The Starzls never seriously considered using lawyers or others as intermediaries, nor would they countenance the presence of "foreigners" in important meetings. In Tim's view, this approach offered distinct advantages for a small company operating within an amorphous regulatory framework. However, as the senior management of PanTheryx shifted to Mark Braman and his more seasoned team of corporate executives, Tim reluctantly acknowledged the inevitability of the new team engaging directly with the dreaded Indian bureaucracy.

During my due diligence work on the company in late 2010, I spoke to a seasoned American pharmaceutical executive who had spent over 20 years in East Asia opening new markets for his employer. After the predictable warnings about product piracy in India, he offered another piece of advice that would resonate with me repeatedly as things progressed: "It's best to move very fast, so the bureaucrats can't keep writing regulations to slow you down."

***

Mark Braman's joining the company as CEO in late 2011 coincided with a significant shift in the Indian regulatory landscape for food products. In 2006, India had passed the Food Safety and Standards Act, consolidating an arcane mosaic of laws and regulations related to food products. The intention was to harmonize India's regulatory framework with those of the United States and Europe. The government established the Food Safety and Standard Authority of India (FSSAI) two years later to implement the new act.

As PanTheryx entered 2012, plans to launch its product in India were ensnared in uncertainty as regulations on nutritional supplements met delays. FSSAI offered no public assurances about specific claims that could be made for these products or whether premarket approval would be necessary. Indian food companies, both large and small, argued vehemently that the act itself granted no authority to require regulatory approval before food supplements could be sold in the market. Two months later, the chairman of FSSAI took the step of requiring premarket approval of all proprietary foods "without a history of safe use" in the country, regardless of their ingredients. Since no such requirement existed in mature markets anywhere in the world, though, the order stood in stark contrast to the idea that India's Food Safety and Standards Act was intended to harmonize Indian food regulations with those of the United States and Europe.

Nutraceutical companies doing business in India charged that this position was arbitrary and unlawful, and was not authorized under the new legislation. Once again, the chairman offered no clear guidelines for compliance. PanTheryx and its Indian legal counsel warily concluded the new directive did not apply to its product, but an April meeting with FSSAI indicated otherwise. The chairman confirmed that he intended to require premarket approval of all "nonstandardized" foods and to establish regulatory standards for each. PanTheryx's product would require premarket approval by "an internal committee." The chairman provided no guidance as to how long this would take or what the precise requirements for approval would be.

Although tempted to ignore the premarket-approval procedure and take the product directly to market, Braman opted for a more cautious approach. The company began preparing an extensive premarket-approval application. In late summer, the company met with the director of new product approval, who described the company's application as comprehensive and ready for submission. He went on to express appreciation for the positive effect the product would have on the health and well-being of children in India.

The application was submitted to FSSAI in late August, followed by a technical review by the Product Screening Committee, in which no issues were raised, no negative comments were made, and no additional information or clarification was requested. With an update from FSSAI promised for January 2013, Braman wrote to the company's shareholders in mid-December that the company "was optimistic that FSSAI will approve the product, as no objections have been raised during the review process." Rather than moving forward to a speedy approval, however, the application languished in a bog of administrative purgatory. In mid-March, Mark and Julie Lindemann met again with the director of new product approval to move the process forward. Mark described the meeting with the director as very cordial: "He gave us a considerable amount of time and answered all of our questions."

According to the director, the product application would have to be reviewed by the newly formed Scientific Review Panel in late April. Mark left the meeting with "a good feeling" about PanTheryx's chances of receiving clearance to market soon. Over a year had passed from the time the company was first apprised of the need for premarket approval, and eight months from the date its application was submitted to FSSAI. In a March 2013 presentation to potential investors in a new round of funding, the company confirmed that it anticipated "a limited launch of the PanTheryx product beginning early in the third quarter of 2013."

In late June, having received no word regarding the Scientific Review Panel, the company directed its Indian counsel to meet again with the director of new product approval. At the meeting, cordial as always, the lawyer was told that the scientific panel was concerned about the safety of bovine colostrum, a principal ingredient in the

PanTheryx product as well as in dozens of other products under review. Ten days later, on July 4, 2013, the company's counsel visited the offices of the scientific panel to hand-deliver an extensive package of information documenting the safety of colostrum. Before she could even deliver it, a clerk peremptorily handed her a one-paragraph letter. It stated that, since DiaResQ was to be used "in severe cases of diarrhea under critical supervision," it would only be permitted in a hospital setting. It added that since the application failed to provide data documenting a history of safe use, the panel recommended not approving the product "as a supplement for special dietary use."

In short, the panel had refused to approve the product on the grounds that it displayed characteristics of a drug rather than a food, apparently rooted in the erroneous idea that it must be administered in a hospital to severely ill patients under supervision. As Mark emphasized in a letter to shareholders, this was "factually incorrect as our product is safely administered in home, clinic, and hospital settings with and without critical supervision and provides benefits to all children suffering from diarrhea, whether mild or severe."

The company's in-house counsel, Scott Hyman, arranged a meeting with the director of new product approval in early September to discuss the decision and seek guidance on addressing it. Hyman was keenly aware going in of India's reputation for bureaucratic lack of accountability in such settings. Then, much to his surprise, Scott was advised that a new director of new product approval had been appointed. Scott later learned from sources in New Delhi that the prior director, with whom the company had met several times and from whom it had gratefully received substantive guidance regarding its application, had been removed from his position "for misconduct."

Signs of progress against bureaucracy and corruption like this came too little, too late for many foreign companies. In October

2013, the *New York Times* reported that Wal-Mart, the second-largest company in the world by revenue, had indefinitely suspended multi-year efforts to open hundreds of stores across India. According to a consultant following the story, Wal-Mart had experienced growing frustration "about the obstacles to doing business with India and the changing configurations of what it could do and what it couldn't do ...To just continue to pump in money without reflecting on this would be pointless."

For PanTheryx, with resources a minuscule fraction of Wal-Mart's, surmounting India's obstacles to its product was more than a matter of prudence; it was crucial to the viability of the company.

9

Bangladesh

Of the new state of Bangladesh, Kissinger remarked coldly that it was "a basket case" before turning his unsolicited expertise elsewhere.

—Christopher Hitchens, *The Trial of Henry Kissinger*

A decisive breakthrough in reducing the death toll of diarrhea had emerged from Bangladesh 40 years before the founding of PanTheryx. Although oral rehydration therapy did not cure the affliction or curtail its duration, it kept the patient alive until the episode subsided. Remarkably, no major therapeutic advance in the treatment of the disease had emerged during this 40-year period.

To appreciate the significance of the invention of DiaResQ, it helps to understand this timeline. The story begins with a tempest in the Indian Ocean. The sixth cyclone of the 1970 fall monsoon season began as a weather disturbance on November 8, gaining mass as thunderstorms fused together, slowly intensifying as they sucked moisture into the atmosphere from the warm waters of the Bay of Bengal. Escalating into a colossal, doughnut-shaped airstream, the new cyclone plodded toward the southern coast of what was then known as East Pakistan.

On November 12, as the eye of the cyclone reached landfall in the low-lying Ganges Delta, the wind-speed on its outer edges exceeded 200 miles per hour. The storm surge hurled a wall of water inland exceeding the height of a three-story building, inundating tens of thousands of square miles of a country where most of the land mass rose less than 10 feet above sea level. In contrast, for example, to the hurricanes that lashed the southeastern United States in 2017, the impoverished farmers, fishermen, and shopkeepers in the path of the surge were given no warning of the impending disaster. No alarms sounded, no evacuation was ordered.

The Bhola Cyclone, as it became known, would go down as the deadliest tropical storm in history. An estimated 500,000 people drowned or were washed to sea as the storm surge receded. Imagine the population of Sacramento or Tucson wiped out in a matter of hours. Yet, in an improbable turn of events, the Bhola Cyclone tragedy became the catalyst for the creation of the country of Bangladesh, as well as for dramatic improvements in health care that would save the lives of millions of children.

How could a cyclone form a new country? The British Empire had reluctantly abandoned its colonial ambitions in the Indian sub-continent in 1947. The region stretching from the Arabian Sea in the west to the Bay of Bengal and Burma (now Myanmar) in the east was partitioned into two countries based on religion. The central bulk of the former colony, predominantly Hindu, was declared India. The areas containing most of the Muslim population became Pakistan: two untethered provinces bracketing northern India. West Pakistan was more prosperous and politically dominant. Smaller, more populous, and destitute East Pakistan sat across 1,200 miles of India to the east. One Indian diplomat concluded the British had created a "geographical monstrosity."

Long-simmering political and economic fissures between the two Pakistani regions boiled over in 1970 when the West Pakistan government essentially ignored the plight of East Pakistan after the Bhola Cyclone, offering only meager assistance. Resentment in East Pakistan led to an election won by nationalists. The province soon declared its independence from West Pakistan, naming itself Bangladesh. Refusing to recognize the newly formed government, West Pakistan launched a brutal military assault on the eastern province in March 1971, leading to a nine-month war for independence. Over 300,000 people were killed in the conflict, and millions of refugees were driven into neighboring India and West Bengal, triggering cholera epidemics in the refugee camps.

At the time, properly treating cholera in conditions like these was considered impossible. Previous trials had demonstrated the potential for rehydration to replace fluids and electrolytes lost during chronic episodes of diarrhea, especially those related to cholera. However, this rehydration was achieved by administering intravenous fluids, an impractical solution in remote or inhospitable conditions.

This barrier was eliminated in 1968 by Dr. Richard Cash and Dr. David Nalen, two Americans working with the Pakistan-SEATO Cholera Research Laboratory in Dhaka, the capital of East Pakistan (now the icddr,b, the world's leading center for diarrheal research). Cash and Nalen published an article in *The Lancet* describing an oral solution containing glucose and salt. Their clinical trials found that this oral rehydration solution could reduce the need for IV treatments in acute cholera cases by 80 percent. "Once we developed a method for giving oral rehydration therapy," Dr. Cash later observed, "it proved to work with all types of diarrhoea, whatever the cause."

As the cholera epidemic began ravaging the refugee camps created by the 1971 War of Liberation, the extraordinary value of ORS was demonstrated for the first time on a large scale. When the supply of intravenous fluids in the refugee camps was depleted, Dr. Dilip Mahalanabis, leading a team of health-care workers and local citizens at a camp with 350,000 refugees, authorized the mixture and administration of ORS. The cholera death rate among those treated with ORS dropped from 30 percent to only 3 percent.

Dr. Mahalanabis later recalled: "We were essentially using people to experiment on. But we were pushed to the wall. We had no choice." Cash and Nalen's breakthrough three years earlier had been confirmed. Oral rehydration therapy would go on to save 50 million lives over the next 50 years.

In the 1980s, a nongovernmental organization, BRAC, organized a brilliant campaign to spread the use of ORS throughout Bangladesh. BRAC enlisted thousands of health workers and volunteers to travel the country teaching people how to mix salt, sugar, and water in the right proportions and administer the resulting solution to children with diarrhea. Thanks to this campaign, 12 million Bangladeshi women were taught how to administer ORS. (Today, BRAC is the largest NGO in the world, providing a wide variety of services, from micro-lending to legal assistance.)

Despite the obstacles the new country faced after the War of Liberation, including several decades of poverty, political turmoil, and recurring droughts, cyclones, and floods, Bangladesh achieved remarkable improvements in the health and well-being of its population, prompting *The Lancet* to declare the transformation "one of the great mysteries of global health." In 2012, *The Economist* reported: "The most dramatic period of improvement in human health in history is often taken to be that of late-nineteenth-century Japan, during the remarkable modernization of the Meiji transition.

Bangladesh's record on child and maternal mortality has been comparable in scale."

With a population of 166 million, more than Russia or Japan, compressed into an area the size of Iowa, Bangladesh is one of the most densely populated countries on earth. Its per capita income is less than half that of India. Yet Bangladesh has outperformed India over the past 30 years in many indicators of health and wellness. Indeed, although it remains one of the poorest countries in the world, Bangladesh has the longest life expectancy and the lowest infant and under-five mortality rates of any country in South Asia.

In a revealing series of articles in November 2013, *The Lancet* attributed much of this success to advances instituted by the Bangladesh government following the War of Liberation, creating "an environment for pluralistic reform in which many participants in the health sector, including non-governmental organizations and the private sector, were allowed to flourish." The journal highlighted the work of one institution as being pivotal to this: icddr,b, for its pioneering work in the treatment of diarrhea.

Attributable in no small part to icddr,b, the overall mortality rate for children less than five years of age in Bangladesh declined by a stunning 75 percent between 1980 and 2011. *The Lancet* noted that "this decline was not accompanied by a corresponding decrease in the incidence of acute diarrheal disease," suggesting that "these achievements seem to have been driven by improved case management."

This trend was accompanied by the emergence of a flourishing pharmaceutical industry in Bangladesh, which now produces 97 percent of the oral rehydration solutions, zinc, and antibiotics sold in the country. When WHO and UNICEF declared that a combination of ORS and zinc would become the internationally accepted standard of care for pediatric diarrhea, the industry saw an opportunity. In 2003, a Bangladesh-based pharmaceutical company, Acme

Laboratories, partnered with icddr,b and the Bill and Melinda Gates Foundation to create a commercially viable consumer product: low-cost zinc tablets. These tablets are now available for sale throughout the country. Mark Braman and the rest of the team at PanTheryx were intrigued by this public-private partnering model.

***

The PanTheryx management team was increasingly convinced that DiaResQ could be the first major advance in the treatment of pediatric diarrhea in underdeveloped countries since the invention of ORS in Bangladesh 40 years earlier. The company's field trials involving over 200 children at clinics in northern India in 2010 and 2011 had confirmed DiaResQ's effectiveness in reducing the duration of an acute diarrhea episode from days to a matter of hours. They also demonstrated the product was safe, with no adverse events having occurred in any of the children.

Though these tests were conducted under close medical supervision by local physicians, in accordance with the Indian clinicians' understanding of best practices in India at the time, the new management team knew any subsequent clinical trials would have to comply with prevailing international standards. The team also recognized that rapidly evolving international standards called for a more hands-off involvement of the company, formalized institutional review, and a more technically rigorous informed consent by patients.

These standards had been widely codified as Good Clinical Practices (GCP). Gaining the recognition of the world health community would require a demonstration of the safety and effectiveness of DiaResQ in robust clinical trials conducted at world-renowned clinics in accordance with these Good Clinical Practices. Going forward, PanTheryx management committed the company to this paradigm.

10

The Bangladesh Trial

The idea to generate antibody targeting rotavirus and E. coli
...simultaneously would be of immense potentialities in
developing countries, as 60 percent of diarrhoeas in children
4 months to 5 years of age are attributed to these two
pathogens.

—Dr. Shafiqul A. Sarker

Confirming the team's commitment to GCP compliance, the company's discussions with scientists, venture capitalists, and NGOs,
including the Bill and Melinda Gates Foundation, made it clear that
only a successful double-blind, placebo-controlled study in a highly
respected clinical environment would conclusively establish the product's efficacy. Mark Braman and his team also anticipated that such
a study would be a prerequisite to securing long-term alliances with
corporate partners or potential acquirers of the company.

In a placebo-controlled study, the test product is administered to
half the subjects while a physically identical product, minus any active
ingredients, is given to the rest. Recipients of product and placebo

are designated randomly. In a double-blind study, neither the clinicians nor the patients know who is getting the placebo and who is receiving the test product. This eliminates any possibility of bias or favoritism skewing the results. Double-blind, placebo-controlled studies are the benchmark for clinical effectiveness, but successfully executing one presents any early-stage company with a logistical challenge. PanTheryx would need a lot of help to make this happen.

Before Mark Braman joined the company in 2011, an early source of guidance in this process was Evan Simpson, a program officer at PATH, a respected nonprofit organization known for fostering collaborations between public, private, and nonprofit entities to develop "lifesaving health technologies with global impact." In August 2011, Simpson had identified icddr,b in Bangladesh as the ideal third-party clinic to conduct a trial. He further suggested Dr. S. A. Sarker, senior scientist at icddr,b and a widely published clinician in the study and treatment of diarrheal disease, as the researcher to lead the study.

Conducting its clinical trial in Bangladesh would present a daunting hurdle. Dhaka, located in the center of the Ganges Delta, is the capital of Bangladesh. With over 15 million residents, and occupying an area about the size of Scranton, Pennsylvania, Dhaka ranks as one of the world's fastest-growing and most densely populated cities. It is also one of the most congested and polluted. Over 400,000 rickshaws—more than in any other city—weave between countless pedestrians, buses, cars, scooters, and motorcycles along impossibly narrow streets. Unremitting traffic jams, exacerbated by the absence of functional traffic signals in over 90 percent of the city's intersections, render any form of public transportation hopeless.

Lacking access to transport, destitute inhabitants settle into slums wedged between high-rise buildings in the city's core so that they can walk to work. The number of inhabitants in the slums of the city has risen dramatically in recent years as peasants, displaced by rising tides in the low-lying coastal areas on the Bay of Bengal, migrate to the city seeking jobs in the flourishing textile manufacturing industry.

The clinic at icddr,b treats thousands of patients with diarrhea each year. Most are children, and many of these children are experiencing persistent acute diarrhea, defined as diarrhea lasting 14 days or more. On its website, icddr,b notes that in 2007, "the hospital treated over 110,000 people, 35,000 of whom would have died if they had not received [its] care."

The clinic's patient population swells during the monsoon season, from early spring to late summer. Lines out the door often extend the length of two football fields. Beginning as early as March, when temperatures rise and the supply of safe drinking water in Dhaka diminishes, a makeshift camp takes shape outside to house the massive overflow of patients. The ramshackle camp, tents supported by bamboo poles, contrasts the clean and orderly wards inside the clinic. Beneath the tents, lit by temporary bulbs hanging from wires, hundreds of patients rest in portable cots set inches apart. Many receive saline solution intravenously from plastic bags hanging from repurposed wire coat hangers.

Evan Simpson was aware that Dr. Sarker had published the results of clinical studies performed at icddr,b over 10 years earlier in which bovine colostrum and chicken egg yolks had been tested individually in separate clinical trials as potential treatments for pediatric diarrhea. Although the trials failed to show a significant impact on the duration of diarrhea episodes, each ingredient appeared to trigger some reduction in stool output. In July 2011, PanTheryx asked Simpson to gauge Dr. Sarker's interest in a collaboration. In an email to Dr. Sarker, Simpson said PATH was aware of "orally administered powdered products" containing bovine colostrum and egg yolks that "may be advancing through the development process, but which need more scientific evidence of efficacy." Without naming PanTheryx, he concluded by suggesting that PATH would be interested in opening a dialogue regarding the potential for a research collaboration "to determine the efficacy of such products in treating non-specific acute diarrhea in children."

Sarker quickly responded: "Because of its potentialities to exert benefit in childhood diarrhea, I still am interested to work in this area." He confirmed that "the area still needs more scientific evidence of efficacy." The doctor also suggested that "the topic of non-specific diarrhea could be of interest for trial," emphasizing the potentially revolutionary impact of a single intervention addressing multiple diarrhea-causing pathogens rather than a single virus or bacterium.

This was a promising response, but for PanTheryx, advancing a dialogue at that point with any scientist outside of the company, even one of Dr. Sarker's reputation, presented problems. Tim Starzl was aware of Dr. Sarker's research and publications around the treatment of pediatric diarrhea, even having cited one of Sarker's papers in the PanTheryx patent filing being prepared. Until the patent was filed in the United States and internationally, however, any disclosures regarding the company's technology and proprietary inventions could endanger its validity. Although Tim continued to work feverishly with the company's patent counsel on the application, it could be months before the filing was completed.

Further, shortly after Simpson's first contact with Dr. Sarker, PanTheryx began the process of recruiting Mark Braman to join the company as CEO. After signing on with the company in late October, Mark would need several months to complete the ongoing round of financing, recruit his own management team, and conduct a thorough review of the company's strategy and business plan. Discussions involving potential clinical trials and other relationships with outside parties would have to be shelved for the time being.

***

By April 2012, as the company struggled to satisfy the changing regulatory requirements to launch the product in India, Mark and Julie Lindemann, the new VP of safety, regulatory, and clinical affairs, reconnected with Evan Simpson and began conversations with Dr. Sarker regarding a clinical trial at icddr,b. Sarker's enthusiasm for pursuing the project intensified as the discussions progressed. He and his associates were treating over 500 pediatric diarrhea patients a day. Over the next several months, Sarker and PanTheryx refined the protocol for a trial as preliminary reviews were conducted by external academic scientists as well as the icddr,b Research and Ethics committees. One sticking point was icddr,b's desire to know the precise composition of the product and how it was produced. Although the PanTheryx final patent application had been filed in November 2011, the company declined to share the requested information on the grounds that it would violate highly sensitive trade secrets.

The PanTheryx team and Dr. Sarker drafted a Clinical Study Protocol stating its objectives: to determine whether three days of DiaResQ added to the standard of care regimen of oral rehydration solutions and zinc would "significantly reduce the duration of the diarrhea episode, impact diarrhea symptoms (stool consistency and frequency), and improve food intake during a seven-day period." To be considered successful, the study would need to reach that bar. The scientific evidence made it clear that diarrhea episodes lasting three days or more, a typical outcome with the standard of care, placed the child's life at risk. As a result, the protocol emphasized that the "primary endpoint" of the study would be reducing the duration of the diarrhea episode.

Protracted discussions centered on how much of a reduction proved DiaResQ's efficacy. Clinical observations of children at icddr,b over decades revealed a consistent average duration for an acute diarrhea episode of 94 hours, or nearly four full days. PanTheryx trial data in India showed that children taking the test product were essentially cured within 24 to 36 hours, a reduction of 62 to 75 percent. Clinicians at icddr,b contended that this result was "impossible," based on all the evidence it had assembled from its previous trials of nutritional products. They requested a more reasonable objective of 35 percent. Since this more modest, although still impressive, objective made the trial only more likely to succeed, PanTheryx accepted the icddr,b rationale. Following receipt of the final committee approvals in February 2013, the company's long-awaited double-blind, placebo-controlled study commenced. Enrollment of the first patient took place on March 14, over one and a half years after Evan Simpson's initial inquiry to Dr. Sarker.

Conscious of the enormous team effort involved in reaching this milestone, Julie emailed the team: "Thanks to you all for help with protocol review, test article and placebo formulation and manufacture, analytical, documents printing, binder collating, shipping, insurance, agreements, relationship building with Dr. Sarker, meeting arrangements and travel, visas, moral support to help make this happen."

Clouding the celebratory mood accompanying the clinical trial, however, was the political and social turmoil on the streets of Dhaka. Lingering embers of resentment stemming back to the 1971 war for independence had again flared to life. As the PanTheryx trial commenced, the Islamist-leaning Bangladesh Nationalist Party, or BNP, joined by the country's largest Islamist party, had been staging increasingly violent protests. Their outrage was directed against a tribunal, established by the ruling Awami League, to prosecute human rights abuses suffered during the 1971 war at the hands of the Pakistani army and local collaborators, many of whom were believed to be fundamentalist Islamists.

Intensifying the bedlam, five weeks after the PanTheryx clinical trial began, Bangladesh experienced the deadliest industrial disaster in its history. An eight-story building on the outskirts of Dhaka— containing five garment factories and employing over 3,000 workers— collapsed. Weeks passed as rescue workers toiled around the clock to rescue the injured from the rubble and to remove the dead. The eventual death toll exceeded 1,100.

The Bangladesh garment industry is the engine of the nation's economy. It generates $20 billion, nearly 80 percent of the nation's total exports, and employs 3.6 million workers, mostly illiterate young women paid the minimum wage of $38 per month. The building collapse focused international attention on poor working conditions in the industry, sparking a wave of protests throughout the year as workers demanded higher wages and enhanced safety standards.

The acrimony spawned by this combination of political confrontations and rebellious factory workers evolved into a "strike culture," as dozens of protests virtually suffocated the country and rendered the daily lives of many of its citizens unbearable. Protest strikes in Bangladesh, known as "hartals," feature a ferocity and scope hard to imagine in most Western countries: hundreds of thousands of people engulf highways and thoroughfares, closing shops, factories, government buildings, and schools. Hartals are often accompanied by widespread violence, including the torching of buses, cars, businesses, and police stations, and resulting in hundreds of senseless deaths. One Dhaka newspaper at the time opined: "This is Bangladesh, a country where normalcy seems a distant dream, and where hartal has become a way of life."

The volatile conditions in Dhaka were hardly conducive to the smooth execution of the PanTheryx clinical trial, which required most families to deliver their infant patients to the hospital via public transportation while being harassed and imperiled by angry mobs.

PanTheryx was also concerned to ensure the safety of Julie and Mark during their visits to icddr,b throughout the course of the trial.

Julie Lindemann arrived in Dhaka in the first week of May to begin monitoring the early trial results. It was at this point, right after a two-week truce between the warring factions in honor of those killed in the garment factory collapse, that a violent hartal raged across the country. As the situation worsened, Dr. Sarker began sending Julie and the other clinicians home early to avoid the worst of the street violence, sometimes arranging to have Julie transported to her hotel by a hospital ambulance to mitigate the chances of being attacked.

Despite the surrounding turbulence, the monitoring itself proceeded smoothly. Although the study was "blinded," meaning no one knew which patients were receiving the test product and which the placebo, the early results were encouraging; a remarkable pattern began to emerge.

Many patients were recovering in 4 to 10 hours, durations never before observed in any such test at icddr,b. The rest were still experiencing acute diarrhea for two or three days. This was, in short, a pattern one might expect to see in a trial involving an intervention that is clearly superior to the placebo. As the indications of a breakthrough grew stronger, Dr. Sarker's professional skepticism slowly dissolved. Over dinner with Mark one night, he admitted, "My expectations are quite high."

During an early fall visit to Dhaka, Mark held a meeting with a leading Bangladesh pharmaceutical company to discuss a potential partnership for distribution of the product. He decided to invite Dr. Sarker, knowing that, in Mark's words, the doctor "was totally revered in the country." Dr. Sarker sat silently as half a dozen pharmaceutical executives grilled Mark, challenging the PanTheryx business model, the efficacy of the product, and the proposed pricing for the

Bangladesh market. Mark became increasingly uneasy and frustrated, as the discussion grew more and more heated.

After several minutes, Sarker politely but firmly interrupted. "Gentlemen," he said, "you do not seem to understand. There is no product that does what this product does. This is a market changer that could have a major impact on our country." He went on to explain how DiaResQ would cause a "major shift" in the treatment of pediatric diarrhea, replacing other products currently in use and leading to a significant reduction in hospital admissions. Sarker concluded by noting that the PanTheryx product could not be compared to the current ORS and zinc standard of care because, unlike ORS and zinc, it reduced the *duration* of the diarrhea episode and "changed the course of the disease." After a moment of silence, one of the executives said, "Well, we've just heard it from the expert." The others nodded their approval, and the dialogue moved on to more substantive aspects of a potential agreement.

As was the case in northern India, Bangladeshi parents were reluctant to miss work or travel long distances on public transportation to visit a hospital, so the pediatric patients admitted to the clinic tended to be extremely sick, "the most serious cases." Also, due to the presence of a more resilient and diverse spectrum of pathogens, pediatric diarrhea cases in Bangladesh were more serious, and thus tougher to treat, than those found in India. Notwithstanding this difference, the recovery patterns seen in the early weeks of the clinical trial continued through the summer monsoon season. In fact, other promising signals emerged as the data from the trial was accumulated and analyzed. For instance, Dr. Sarker reported "conclusive and very compelling" data confirming that the product was "safe." No negative side effects were identified, even in cases involving cholera or other complications. This was significant because the product was treating "undifferentiated" cases, meaning all patients would receive the treatment without being prescreened.

Another endpoint being monitored as a safety parameter related to an increase or decrease in vomiting. Vomiting was known to be a significant contributor to dehydration, making the administration of ORS and food to patients more challenging. The trial data suggested that many patients experienced a dramatic decrease in vomiting, especially in cases involving rotavirus and cholera. Dr. Sarker considered this trend, should it continue, to be significant for public health policy. The product might allow early treatment of patients suspected of having cholera before the diagnosis could be confirmed.

The last patient in the icddr,b clinical trial was enrolled on September 18, 2013, coinciding with another violent strike called by the hardline Islamist party in reaction to a supreme court decision sentencing their leader to death for crimes committed during the war with Pakistan. As buses and trucks around Dhaka were being attacked and burned by demonstrators, communications with Dr. Sarker were temporarily halted, slowing the evaluation of the final patients as the clinical trial wound to a close.

On October 22, Dr. Sarker was on a flight from Dhaka to Orlando, where he would attend a pediatric conference for three days. While he was in the air, Julie nervously awaited the initial unblinded results of the clinical trial from the independent Contract Research Organization. CRO had monitored the trial and collected the data.

When the results arrived, Julie was bewildered. The PanTheryx product had performed as expected, reducing diarrhea episodes to an average duration of 29 hours, essentially duplicating the results from the trials in India. This was the outcome icddr,b had deemed impossible: a 70 percent reduction of the 94-hour duration expected based on three decades of prior studies. The product had demolished the 35 percent reduction goal in the trial protocol.

The source of Julie's consternation was the placebo. The data showed that the average duration of diarrhea episodes for patients taking the placebo was 32 hours, a statistically insignificant difference. If the data held true, the results would be declared "equivocal," dealing a crippling blow to the company's fundraising efforts and corporate partner negotiations. As the management team abruptly shifted its focus from optimistic sales pitches to damage control, the future of the company, once again, hung in the balance.

11

Staying the Course

In times of difficulty, those brave enough to stay the course
will be victors in the end.
                    —Bo Schembechler, head football coach,
                                University of Michigan

When the icddr,b clinical trial began in March 2013, results were
expected by mid-summer. As slower than expected enrollment,
higher than predicted disqualifications of patients from cholera and
other complications, and increasingly violent hartals on the streets
of Dhaka prolonged the trial into the fall months, a positive
outcome became increasingly critical to sustain the company's
forward momentum.

My inbox swelled with polite inquiries regarding the clinical trial
from members of the Leather Apron Club, and I shuttled between
the investors and the management team, striving—tactfully—to
manage expectations. My task required an extra measure of discretion;

I was one of the few who knew that the company was running out of cash.

In early 2013, Mark Braman launched a $10-million financing round, valuing the company at more than $50 million. This was a lofty goal for a company that had generated no revenue. The aggressive valuation reflected a sanguine belief that this would be a breakout year for PanTheryx, anticipating commercial introduction of the product in Mexico and India, execution of the first of several anticipated corporate partnership agreements, and a successful double-blind, placebo-controlled clinical trial in Bangladesh.

Despite a series of optimistic meetings, a persistent lack of good news brought financing to a standstill. Several promising investor prospects withheld financial commitments pending positive news from Bangladesh.

In early July, Indian regulatory authorities unexpectedly denied the company's application for approval to sell DiaResQ, consigning the company's largest potential market to an indefinite holding pattern. George voiced the team's frustration with the regulatory delays in India and elsewhere: "It seems crazy that we have a product that works so well that regulators hold it against us."

Failure to gain approval to market the product in India underscored the increasing importance of a timely and successful launch in the next country selected by PanTheryx to generate early revenue: Mexico. PanTheryx's drive to enter the Mexican market had begun during conversations with John Conley and Craig Johnson, successful Denver entrepreneurs who would become key members of the Leather Apron Club.

Conley grew up on a ranch near Pueblo, Colorado. His father owned a meat-packing business. Although John's father thought of his five kids as "ranch hands" and treated them accordingly, in most respects John enjoyed an idyllic western childhood. Upon graduation from high school in Colorado Springs, John secured an appointment to the Air Force Academy; after two years, he transferred to the University of Colorado Boulder. His free-spirited love of the west had convinced him that he "just wasn't cut out for the military."

After graduating in 1967, John landed a job with Kaiser Steel, which sent him to Fontana, California, a town not far from Los Angeles. Working in the largest steel plant in the western United States, John made his way up to the position of senior melter (the floor manager responsible for making the steel). He was the youngest person to reach that level in the plant's history. Although basking in success with increasing pay and responsibility, John hated the traffic congestion in southern California and longed to return to Colorado. When he told his boss his decision to resign, Edgar Kaiser, the company's chairman, summoned John to the Oakland headquarters.

"Kid," he told John, "you're making a hell of a mistake." John refused to back down. Kaiser, recognizing the unique skill and knowledge John had acquired as a senior melter, offered to continue paying his salary for two years if he would sign a noncompete contract agreeing to "have nothing to do with the steel industry." John eagerly executed the document and headed for Denver.

Over the next 25 years, Conley built and sold several industrial enterprises, some in Mexico. Along with his partner, Craig Johnson, a successful Colorado real estate developer, investor, and philanthropist, Conley invested in a casino business in Mexico City. By 2011, Conley and Johnson had developed a strong web of business relationships in Mexico.

John and Craig invested in PanTheryx in the fall of 2011, just as Mark Braman assumed the CEO role at the company. "We didn't know the first thing about the business," Conley later told me. Like so many other members of the PanTheryx Leather Apron Club, John and Craig were astute businesspeople who were also big-hearted.

They readily admitted that the potential for PanTheryx to ease the lives of poor children in rural areas of underdeveloped countries made the investment especially appealing. Alongside their casino operations, John and Craig ran a charity assisting hospitals in Mexico. To launch the effort, they partnered with Project C.U.R.E., a Denver-based humanitarian relief organization recognized as the largest provider of donated medical supplies and equipment to developing countries around the world.

Through their combined efforts, the partnership had been responsible for the donation of over $23 million of equipment and supplies to 31 hospitals in Mexico. This affiliation would evolve into a strong working relationship between Project C.U.R.E and PanTheryx in the years ahead.

PanTheryx's efforts to enter Mexico are emblematic of the difficulties the company endured across international markets, and in a broader sense, of the challenges faced by entrepreneurs leading early-stage companies. With Conley's assistance, Braman was introduced to Grupo Bruluart, a fast-growing, family-owned, Mexican pharmaceutical manufacturer and distributor. From discussions with management beginning in May 2012, Bruluart appeared to have the characteristics of an ideal partner. In addition to its focus on pediatric products, the company owned 1,500 proprietary pharmacies and 100 distribution centers servicing an additional 30,000 independent pharmacies. Most Bruluart-owned pharmacies had a doctor on-site who could recommend the product to customers, a model the company claimed was unique to Mexico.

In June 2012, Bruluart advised PanTheryx that the regulatory process—getting the label approved by COFEPRIS, the Mexican equivalent of the FDA, and obtaining the appropriate import license—would take no more than 90 days. Management felt comfortable estimating that Conforta 1•2•3—the product's name in

Mexico and the Latin American markets—would go on sale by October. (Signs were created for Mexican pharmacies with the tagline *El Mejor Amigo para la Pancita!* or Tummy's best friend!)

On the contrary, an excruciating series of delays in dealing with regulators and negotiating the final details of the agreement with Bruluart would follow. In fact, it would be early November 2012, not long after the company filed its FSSAI premarket approval application in India, before PanTheryx and Bruluart signed an agreement giving Bruluart's distribution division, Brudifarma, exclusive rights to distribute Conforta 1•2•3 in Mexico for five years.

Less than a month later, Mexico's new president, Enrique Peña Nieto, took office, promising sweeping regulatory reforms and a more centralized government. By January 2013, key personnel at COFEPRIS were being replaced by the new administration. The target for approval of the product's classification was pushed to April, with a formal product launch in Mexico by May. In late August, COFEPRIS finally granted formal regulatory classification of Conforta 1•2•3 as a food supplement. The company immediately began preparing the application for a Sanitary Import Permit and commenced discussions with Mexico customs officers to ensure that the customs classification of the product would be consistent with the COFEPRIS classification.

In late November 2013, more than 12 months after the agreement with Bruluart had been signed, the team expressed cautious optimism that a product launch in Mexico was imminent. Yet more obstacles and delays lay ahead.

***

As Mark Braman and his team increasingly dominated the strategic and operational expansion of the company, Tim Starzl's involvement in day-to-day management decisions waned. Inevitably, this led to differences between Tim and the rest of the team. Tension within the company became an annoying distraction for all concerned.

As an impartial director who admired everyone involved, I did my best to ameliorate these differences. I wasn't at all surprised, however, to see the company going through this phase. Since the venture capital model for funding early-stage companies became entrenched in the 1960s, contentious relationships between founders and seasoned managers have been a common theme. Although thousands of early-stage companies have been funded, relatively few can claim to have been wildly successful under the long-term leadership of a founder who retained the CEO title. Microsoft, Apple, and Facebook make this claim but, beyond these remarkable successes, the list trails off fast.

Visionary founders are creative, intelligent, and driven. Typically, they have spent most of their careers experimenting and innovating. What they have rarely done is invest much time in developing strong leadership and management skills.

Every aspect of Tim Starzl, physical and intellectual, can be characterized in one word: large. Undeniably brilliant, Tim has a tendency to make other people feel positively dormant by comparison. When he gets started on an idea, he can talk a mile a minute, often interrupting himself: "I'm talking too much, aren't I?" or "Would you rather we discuss this at another time?"

Aristotle believed that mastery of metaphor was a sign of genius. Tim personified this assertion. His presentations were rife with metaphors drawn from literature, historic battles, current news and entertainment, and every other topic or source imaginable. For others in the room trying to tackle the mundane issues on the meeting's agenda, these discourses could be entertaining, distracting, confusing, astute, and informative—all at the same time.

A close observer of Dr. Thomas Starzl, Tim's father, wrote that anyone who worked with the legendary surgeon would "admit without hesitation that he is the most perplexing, frustrating, driven, argumentative—and brilliant—human being they have ever encountered." Having the opportunity to work closely with Tim over an extended period, I found the similarities between Tim and his father hard to ignore.

Beyond any tensions among members of the team, Tim was becoming increasingly excited by the idea of pursuing new creative collaborations with his son, Ravi, now a professor and rising star in computer science at Carnegie Mellon. What's more, Bimla had been experiencing health problems for almost a year, limiting her role at the company and placing an increasing burden on Tim as a caretaker.

In late summer 2013, Tim and Bimla decided the time had come to leave the company and move on. By September, separation agreements had been executed and the Starzls formally departed PanTheryx. The patent having been filed and the efficacy of the product demonstrated, Tim's departure was not expected to have a major impact as the company shifted into the execution phase of its production and marketing plans.

That said, the Starzls' departure in the midst of challenging events elicited concerns from investors. "Losing the firm's intellectual property generator seems problematic," one said. Ironically, shortly after the departure of Tim and Bimla, the company was issued its first patent, by Yemen.

***

As Boulder observed the twelfth anniversary of 9/11, rain began falling in the late afternoon. The downpour gained momentum and intensity. Boulder received over nine inches of precipitation in the next 24 hours, nearly doubling the prior rainfall record for the area. The torrent continued uninterrupted for the next four days, the National Weather Service going so far as to label it biblical in scope. Boulder and the front range of Colorado experienced the worst flooding in memory, an event experts called a once-in-a-millennium event.

Though following the progress of the Bangladesh clinical trial, Mark Braman had continued pursuing new investors and corporate partners as potential distributors. On September 12, Mark returned to Boulder from a 10-day, 18,000-mile journey to the Philippines, Thailand, Indonesia, and Bangladesh. Leaving behind the last of the monsoon season in Southeast Asia, he found his hometown in Colorado swamped by a monsoon greater than any he had encountered on his trips to East Asia over the past two years.

The PanTheryx office, on the second floor of a drab stucco building in an office park on the east side of town, was spared any damage from the flood. However, the impact on the surrounding area was calamitous. Over 2,000 homes and 500 miles of roads were destroyed or severely damaged. Nine people died, some swept away as they tried to escape their stranded automobiles.

PanTheryx director Dave Cook's house was in Lyons, one of the towns hit hardest. He and his wife couldn't return home and spent the next several weeks staying in hotels or with friends.

Back in his office and out of the rain, Mark reengaged with the challenges presented by India, Mexico, the Starzls' departure, and the company's financing. Notwithstanding some recent setbacks, based on the analysis of the encouraging blinded data being harvested from the Bangladesh clinical trial through the summer months, management had struggled to restrain its exuberant anticipation of an affirmative outcome. An infusion of positive news from Bangladesh would refocus the company and instill renewed optimism in the investors.

But contrary to management's fervent hopes, the confusing results from the Bangladesh trial drained much of the enthusiasm. After directing the trial monitors to rerun the numbers to assure their accuracy, Julie huddled with the management team to begin formulating a strategy to discern what might have gone wrong and how the company would define and implement measures to contain the damage.

By the time Dr. Sarker reached his hotel in Orlando to attend a medical conference, a lengthy email from Julie awaited him, seeking clarification on several aspects of the trial and prior icddr,b studies. After reviewing the data, Dr. Sarker adopted a positive interpretation of the results, emphasizing he had "never seen anything that delivered these kinds of results" in treating diarrhea, while continuing to express his surprise and disappointment with the "unprecedented findings" with the placebo.

Sarker subsequently sent an encouraging confirmation to the company, which Mark shared with investors and employees: "I am pleased and very encouraged by the outcome of the study. In my experience, children with acute diarrhea generally recover on average a minimum of 72 hours after receiving ORS and zinc. With a mean duration of 29 hours, DiaResQ showed approximately 200–300% improvement in duration over the ORS/zinc standard of care."

Mindful of the 50-year hiatus in search of breakthrough solutions to halt diarrhea, Dr. Sarker concluded, "In my opinion, DiaResQ is the best intervention for diarrhea that we have tested in our facility." With regard to the placebo, he noted, "This was a totally unexpected and, at this point, an inexplicable result."

The placebo used in a double-blind clinical study is, by definition, an "inert substance that is used to hide the genuine treatment." Ideally, the placebo should resemble the test product in appearance and taste. Studies confirm that in many instances patients experience beneficial effects from placebos, a phenomenon known as the "placebo effect," based on being treated in a caring, empathetic environment and the expectation that a legitimate treatment is being administered. The placebo used in the icddr,b study contained dried milk in a formulation used by Dr. Sarker in many previous studies, evincing no relief or positive benefit to the patients.

Further, because many of the patients in the PanTheryx study were three years old or younger and seriously ill, the likelihood of the patient comprehending the care being administered was greatly diminished. Somewhat worrisome, however, was the appearance of the placebo, which upon careful examination could be distinguished from the genuine product.

The challenge facing the company was to figure out why the study didn't work and how to fix it. Optimism among company employees remained relatively strong. "No one said 'Oh my gosh, the product doesn't work,'" Scott Hyman pointed out. C. S. Wee, the company's local representative in East Asia, was similarly optimistic, writing to Mark: "We should take great comfort in the fact that the product has proven its safety and efficacy in a double-blinded placebo trial, and under the supervision of a renowned researcher in this area."

An exhaustive investigation was launched as team members retraced every step of the process, including the production and packaging of the test material and the placebo, the randomization of the packages, the labeling of the packages, the storage and handling of the packages at the clinic, and the detailed logs recording administration of the product and the placebo in the hospital ward. The team also began a meticulous search of the scientific literature for every diarrhea study dating back several decades at icddr,b, as well as at other clinical sites around the world, to determine if any placebo ever used in a similar study had a beneficial effect on patients.

The company's research revealed 38 studies, 14 of which took place at icddr,b, whose study populations and entry criteria were similar to the PanTheryx study. The research confirmed the average diarrhea duration across all 38 studies for patients who received only ORS, with or without zinc, was 95 hours. In other words, there appeared to be no credible evidence that the placebo could have any effect as an anti-diarrheal treatment. But taking no chances, the company filed a provisional patent covering the placebo formulation.

A report from the company to investors read: "Had the average diarrhea duration of the DiaResQ group and the placebo group been consistent with historically reported trials conducted at icddr,b (i.e., 72–139 hours), one could conclude that DiaResQ did not work." On the other hand, the fact that both the product and the placebo worked with such dramatic reductions in duration was an astonishing, albeit confusing, result.

The company's detective work continued well into November, producing no logical explanation of what might have gone wrong. In the meantime, investors and others who learned of the outcome did not shrink from sharing their opinions. Many speculated that workers in the clinic ward had ascertained which packets contained DiaResQ based on the appearance or positive impact of some packets, and, out of compassion, provided them to the sickest infants. "I think it would be hard for a caring nurse (probably a mother herself) to give the miracle powder to an obviously healthy infant while the baby beside it is suffering terribly," one investor wrote.

Rather than celebrating a successful conclusion to the highly anticipated 2013 "breakout year," PanTheryx was instead confronting a crucible of ambiguity and apprehension. The inconclusive results from the Bangladesh trial combined with the Indian regulators' abrupt denial of premarket approval to market DiaResQ in India, continuing regulatory delays in Mexico, and the erratic responses to the fundraising effort would require a thorough recalibration of the company's business plan.

The second anniversary of Mark Braman's joining the company as CEO passed unnoticed on October 3. Despite the recent setbacks, Mark's optimism was unwavering. Intent on preserving the company's focus and momentum, he made it his duty to ensure the rest of the team collectively shared his positive outlook.

As the frenetic year crept toward its dispiriting conclusion, Mark wrote to the PanTheryx team that his "perspective on many things in life has been shaped by an incredible man, Bo Schembechler." He offered a memorable quote from his one-time football coach at Michigan: "In times of difficulty, those brave enough to stay the course will be victors in the end." Looking toward 2014, Mark labeled the trial "a bump in the road" and exhorted the employees of PanTheryx: "If we all stay the course and remain fully committed, we will persevere."

12

The Elephant in the Room

The stuff works. Anyone who has ever taken it knows there
is magic in this little pouch. That's what keeps us going.
—Scott Hyman, Senior Vice President and
General Counsel, PanTheryx

As 2014 began, the PanTheryx management team grappled with a
mosaic of complex challenges. Endless fundraising meetings swamped
Mark's calendar as the company's cash position remained stubbornly
low. Mutable regulatory schemes and bureaucratic maneuvers in countries around the world confounded the company's lawyers and
management. Negotiations with more than a dozen potential corporate
partners headquartered in various time zones demanded attention 24
hours a day. Through it all, discussions with contract manufacturers,
egg producers, colostrum sources, and packaging plants required
coordination as the importance of high-quality, low-cost, and reliable
production became increasingly apparent.

The onus of orchestrating this relentless frenzy of activity fell on a sparse management team consisting of Mark, George, Rob, and Scott. When I asked George how he managed the brutal, round-the-clock schedule, he replied: "I sleep with one eye open." The company's total headcount still only amounted to 14.

On the second day of January, tragic news beset the company. Craig Johnson, a loyal member of the original Leather Apron Club who had been instrumental in facilitating the company's entry into Mexico, had died of a massive heart attack at 53. The obituary in the *Denver Post* observed: "His generous spirit and calling to make a difference extended beyond family and friends. He traveled to some of the poorest and most remote parts of the world, where he worked to heal and shelter people in need."

After attending a standing-room-only memorial service for Craig in Denver on January 6, the PanTheryx management team retreated to the Boulder office, more determined than ever to rekindle the company's positive momentum. The United States economy transitioned smoothly into 2014, continuing a recovery from the recession President Obama had inherited five years earlier. All the major U.S. stock indices surged into record territory as one of the longest bull markets since the 1929 crash continued to astound market watchers and delight investors. From March 2009 through mid-2014, the Obama Bull Market, as some market watchers named it, had risen over 250 percent. Notwithstanding the auspicious financial environment, fundraising for PanTheryx remained a sluggish pursuit.

Even Mother Nature intervened. The week of February 10, Mark, George, and Scott landed in New York City for three days of back-to-back meetings with potential investors and corporate partners. By February 13, over 6,500 flights had been canceled along the east coast due to record snowfall. Businesses closed and the city ground to a standstill. Idle workers cross-country skied down Fifth Avenue.

Obviously, all the meetings had to be canceled. Cloistered in their hotel rooms until they could book flights back to Colorado at the end of the week, the team worked the phones, hoping to make the most of an otherwise lost week.

As the PanTheryx team expanded its research into the regulatory requirements for the sale of DiaResQ in dozens of developing counties, it confronted a bewildering array of regulations and standards. Over the relatively short span of the company's existence, globalization of business opportunities had mushroomed. "Developing" countries evolved into "emerging" countries and "emerging" countries became "growth markets." China typified the trend, rapidly transitioning from an emerging country to the world's second leading pharmaceutical market.

In order to participate in the economic opportunities proliferating alongside globalization, countries with little or no regulatory framework sought to upgrade rules and regulations to be more closely aligned with international standards employed by the developed countries of North America and Europe. Among those attempting to gain a foothold in these markets were pharmaceutical and health-care companies. The concept of harmonizing regulatory schemes across the emerging and developed market countries assumed increasing relevance. Particularly in the category of food-based products for health care, as PanTheryx had learned in India, statutory and regulatory standards were unpredictable at best.

Simply identifying the appropriate category for DiaResQ presented a challenge, in part because no comparable product had been marketed. Depending on the jurisdiction, DiaResQ was classified as a "medical food," a "food supplement," a "dietary supplement," a "food for special dietary use," a "food for special dietary needs of children," a "food for children suffering from diarrhea," and more. Each category entailed different constraints on the contents of product labels, including the product name and types of claims that could be made regarding its use and effectiveness. Most crucial for PanTheryx was that the product not be categorized as a drug, as this would unleash a more onerous, expensive, and time-consuming set of prerequisites to approval.

The FDA is among the most stringent food and drug regulatory agencies in the world. In one of the ironies of the PanTheryx journey, the United States, the country *least* desperately in need of DiaResQ, emerged as the most welcoming environment for marketing the product. When an American company wants to export a food-based medical product to a foreign country, the destination country wants to know if the product can be legally sold in the United States. In order to satisfy this query, the FDA issues a Certificate of Free Sale advising the exporting company, as well as other interested parties, that its food or dietary supplement "may be legally marketed in the United States."

In 2013, the FDA granted PanTheryx two Certificates of Free Sale for DiaResQ: as a Dietary Supplement to "support intestinal health" and as a Food for Special Dietary Use for "occasional diarrhea relief." By May 2014, in addition to the United States, PanTheryx had been cleared to sell its products in American Samoa, Mexico, Singapore, Malaysia, and Brunei. In March, the company shipped its first order to American Samoa, where the product would be sold under the name TaufaleMalu1-2-3. Because of its size and proximity, however, Mexico remained the destination of highest priority for the time being.

***

The North American Free Trade Agreement (NAFTA), enacted in 1994, was expected to largely eradicate barriers to trade between the United States, Mexico, and Canada. Having obtained Certificates of Free Sale for its product in the United States, PanTheryx was optimistic that clearing Conforta 1•2•3 for export to its neighbor to the south would be quick and painless. Instead, it encountered months of red tape, fluctuating regulations, and extravagant bureaucratic delays.

Traversing 1,500 miles from north to south in the center of the United States, Interstate Highway 35 begins at Duluth, Minnesota, in the north and ends at a stoplight in Laredo, Texas, less than a mile from the Rio Grande River on the United States–Mexico border. In early March 2014, a truck carrying a pallet of 15,000 units of Conforta 1•2•3 traveled south on Highway 35 toward Laredo. The largest inland port in the United States, Laredo teems with warehouses, shipping facilities, and customs brokers to smooth passage of the over $70 billion in commerce crossing the border in both directions each year—not to mention vast quantities of illegal cocaine, marijuana, heroin, guns, and currency, only a small fraction of which is confiscated by United States Customs and Border Protection officials.

Manufactured by APS BioGroup in Phoenix, the Conforta 1•2•3 shipment to Laredo would be held in a PanTheryx customs broker's warehouse pending clearance to enter Mexico. Once cleared by customs officials, the product would move across the border to a Brudifarma warehouse located less than two miles away on the Mexican side of the border.

As newly elected Mexican president Enrique Peña Nieto settled into office, customs and taxation officials, as well as the regulations they enforced, entered a state of flux. In an effort to reduce corruption, the president assigned the Mexican military to control customs enforcement at the border. The presence of the military heightened the level of apprehension among customs brokers and businesspeople on both sides. Preparation of accurate and comprehensive documentation became a paramount concern. PanTheryx management stood by helplessly as its customs broker struggled to monitor the latest regulatory permutations.

PanTheryx had been advised by its brokers and others that its Certificate of Free Sale, which had been issued by the FDA with a two-year term, would be sufficient to allow the smooth transfer of Conforta 1•2•3 through customs into Mexico. Clearance would require approval by COFEPRIS. After examining the certificate, a staff person at COFEPRIS replied that his office only dealt with "one-year Certificates of Free Sale," although why the term of the certificate mattered was anyone's guess. Another official noted that the initials "USA" were entered in the wrong spot on a form and that the import permit application would have to be resubmitted.

Contrary to the position previously taken by COFEPRIS, a staff person at another department insisted that, in addition to the Certificate of Free Sale, PanTheryx would be required to submit a certificate from the United States Department of Agriculture Animal and Plant Health Inspection Service (APHIS) documenting that the animals from which the product was derived had been raised in sanitary conditions.

The unique contents of the product posed additional challenges when it was determined that APHIS had a standard application form for milk and one for eggs, but no form for a mixture of the two. This distinction was crucial, as the importation of dairy products alone was heavily taxed by Mexico. Once a formula solution was devised for the certificate, the company was advised for the first time that a matching certificate would be required from Mexico's agriculture ministry, SAGARPA.

APHIS Certificates were issued in the name of companies that manufacture products, causing more confusion because APS

BioGroup manufactured the product, which was then sold under the PanTheryx name. More time was squandered as the company obtained a letter from APS affirming that it was the "manufacturer" while PanTheryx was the "exporter" of the product. The names of both companies would appear on the label.

Precise timing became an issue as well. Each APHIS Certificate lasted only 30 days, meaning that if other necessary certificates and permits were not issued and effective within that time frame, an application would have to be submitted for a new APHIS Certificate. Since that process could take several days, other certificates and permits might then expire, and the entire drill would have to be repeated. Two months elapsed since the first pallet of Conforta 1•2•3 had arrived in Laredo, and there was no end in sight.

Once the final import permit was issued, Mexico required that the product cross the border on the day of issuance. At one point, the permit was issued but, before the product reached the border, new software being implemented by Mexican customs crashed and the product could not be recorded as "accepted" in time. Again, the process had to be repeated.

At the outset of the company's initiative to ship product into Mexico, PanTheryx management had advised brokers and other parties that the company would under no circumstances pay any form of bribe to facilitate the process. After several months, Mark concluded, without regret, the repeated last-minute delays and arbitrary demands "were because we haven't paid any side money to anyone."

Finally, on June 19, 2014, after the PanTheryx product had inhabited the broker's warehouse for three months, Rob Driver, the vice president of manufacturing, gleefully emailed everyone in the company: "We received confirmation this afternoon that our initial shipment (15,000 units) of Conforta 1•2•3 to Brudifarma has now cleared customs in Mexico and is in transit to the Brudifarma ware-house." Another frustrating chapter in the PanTheryx odyssey came to a close at last.

***

The original business model for marketing DiaResQ in India involved hiring a local sales force of several hundred employees to launch the product in a populous urban region of the country. Once the product proved to be effective and accepted in that locality, the company would use the initial momentum to attract and sign domestic distributors or pharmaceutical companies to expand sales throughout the country.

Although intuitively compelling, in practice this model proved overly complex. The company acknowledged that, as a startup American company, hiring and managing hundreds of employees in underdeveloped countries on the other side of the planet was neither realistic nor feasible.

Following the arrival of Mark Braman and the new management team in late 2011, PanTheryx management began to shift its strategy to establishing relationships with the foremost pharmaceutical com-panies in each country. In addition to having large, well-trained sales organizations of their own, these partners employed in-house regula-tory experts familiar with local filing requirements and bureaucratic procedures for approval of new health-care products.

The PanTheryx management team was pleasantly surprised by the high-level interest in DiaResQ they found at leading pharmaceutical companies. Dismissing the need to demonstrate sales momentum in a smaller market, these companies expressed immediate interest in distributing the product based on three factors: pediatric diarrhea was an enormous unsolved crisis in the countries where they were doing business; a product that claimed to end a diarrheal episode in a matter of hours had never been available to them; and, at first blush, the extraordinary results of the initial field trials in India in 2010 through 2012 were sufficient to substantiate the likely safety and effectiveness of the product.

The seminal partnership signed with Brudifarma in Mexico, although disappointing due to constant delays and poor execution on Brudifarma's part, provided a template for discussions with potential partners in other countries. Representing the world's largest potential market for DiaResQ, India became the company's top priority for the establishment of a robust corporate partner relationship. PanTheryx focused its attention on Dr. Reddy's Laboratories Ltd., India's largest and most respected homegrown pharmaceutical company.

Dr. Reddy's Laboratories had been founded in 1984 by Dr. Kallam Anji Reddy, the son of a turmeric farmer in the state of Andhra Pradesh on India's southeastern coast. Widely credited with being the father of India's modern pharmaceutical industry, Reddy was an entrepreneur, business executive, and philanthropist who, among his many honors, had been awarded the Padma Bhushan, India's third-highest civilian award.

Although his parents had little formal education, Dr. Reddy wrote: "They were clear that I needed a good education. That was their greatest gift to me." Earning a doctorate in chemical engineering, Reddy started his company with only $45,000. Less than 30 years later, the company's annual revenue was approaching $2 billion, making Dr. Reddy one of India's wealthiest citizens. Notwithstanding his renown as an entrepreneur and business executive, Dr. Reddy was perhaps even more revered in India for his humanitarian work focused on promoting child nutrition and bringing sanitary drinking water to rural areas. Based on this combination of factors, the PanTheryx management team concluded Dr. Reddy's Laboratories would be the ideal partner.

Hearing that PanTheryx was looking for senior-level introductions to Indian pharmaceutical companies, John Conley introduced Mark Braman to his brother-in-law, David Mulford, who had served as the United States ambassador to India from 2004 to 2009. Mulford had been acquainted with Dr. Reddy during his years of service in India and offered to arrange the introduction. In March 2013, as Mark was preparing to fly to India to meet with the illustrious gentleman, Dr. Reddy died of cancer at age 72. Mindful of Dr. Reddy's personal interest in pursuing the relationship, other senior executives stepped in to initiate discussions between the two companies shortly thereafter.

The key contact and negotiator for Dr. Reddy's was Alok Sonig, senior vice president and India business head. Sonig would become an enthusiastic supporter and close ally of PanTheryx in the years ahead. After a series of meetings between the management teams, accompanied by intensive research and due diligence by Dr. Reddy's into the science and the market for DiaResQ, in late June 2014 PanTheryx and Dr. Reddy's signed a long-term agreement in which Dr. Reddy's assumed responsibility for the sales, marketing, and distribution of the product throughout India.

Upon hearing a deal had been executed, David Mulford congratulated Mark, writing, "I think you have cut an extremely impressive deal, not just for PanTheryx but also for India." Mark and the rest of his team at PanTheryx were particularly impressed with the "no-nonsense, Western style" of the Dr. Reddy's Laboratories management team. Alok Sonig and the rest of the team had seen "very few opportunities left for major breakthrough products" in the Indian market. They considered the PanTheryx product such an opportunity, going so far as to suggest it could be marketed as "an alternative to antibiotics."

The signing of the agreement with Dr. Reddy's coincided with a significant shift in India's political landscape toward a more business-friendly administration. Narendra Modi, a former tea seller from a lower-caste family in western India, who had campaigned on a pro-business, anti-corruption platform, was swept into office as the new prime minister in a historic victory for his Bharatiya Janata Party.

PanTheryx management expressed cautious optimism that India might perhaps emerge as an accommodating environment for doing business. Indeed, one expert confirmed: "It's going to create a certain sense of stability—U.S. companies are very excited," suggesting Modi would govern as a "pragmatist who wants to show India is 'open for business.'"

On the heels of the Modi victory, another glimmer of positive news arrived from India. Regulatory authorities at FSSAI had called for PanTheryx to obtain premarket approval before DiaResQ could be sold in India. At the end of June, as if tacitly acknowledging the significance of the new agreement with Dr. Reddy's, the Bombay High Court ruled that FSSAI did not have the authority to demand a premarket approval. Scott Hyman advised the PanTheryx board that "we could not have asked for a more favorable decision." The company anxiously awaited news of whether FSSAI would appeal the Bombay High Court decision to the India Supreme Court.

Meanwhile, PanTheryx continued to schedule meetings with NGOs, regulatory bodies, and potential investors and corporate partners through the first half of 2014. The equivocal results from the icddr,b clinical trial in Bangladesh, however, shrouded the otherwise positive discussions, becoming the proverbial elephant in the room. Rather than elide the icddr,b trial results, management channeled the dialogue in a more upbeat direction, emphasizing Dr. Sarker's enthusiasm about the results as well as secondary outcomes from the trial, persuasive evidence that the product was not only safe but also increased food intake and reduced vomiting.

Frustrations grew as a steady stream of anecdotal stories testifying to the product's remarkable effectiveness in both children and adults flowed into the company from around the world. The company's lawyers, accountants, and consultants in India, all of whom had been given a supply of DiaResQ, reported sharing it with ailing family and friends visiting India from other countries, all of whom were cured within hours. One lawyer kept a bowl filled with packets of DiaResQ in her house, welcoming visitors to help themselves. She found herself regularly asking the company to replenish the contents of the bowl.

During negotiations with a large international pharmaceutical company, PanTheryx had provided company executives with samples of DiaResQ for study. The medical director of the company's emerging markets division gave one dose to his young daughter, who had been experiencing an acute infectious diarrhea episode for several days. The child was cured within two hours. "This is a product we must market in every country where we do business," the executive later declared.

Mark spoke for the entire team when he said that "these are the kinds of stories that make it all worthwhile." Scott Hyman observed that the team was motivated by one belief: "The stuff works. Anyone who has ever taken it knows there is magic in this little pouch. That's what keeps us going."

Another potential bright spot for PanTheryx emerged in late summer, when one of the company's cadre of informal supporters, Dr. Mark Grabowsky, offered to nominate DiaResQ for a prestigious international innovation award. Grabowsky, who held the august title "chief operating officer of the Office of the United Nations Special Envoy for Financing the Health Millennium Development Goals and for Malaria," was a renowned medical doctor and global public health expert. Upon being briefed on the PanTheryx product in early 2014, Grabowsky, who had spent many years leading efforts to eradicate malaria in underdeveloped countries, concluded that "this product will have the same effect for diarrhea as bed nets have had for Malaria."

Through his UN work, Grabowsky was aware of a program launched by PATH, the international health organization that had connected PanTheryx with Dr. Sarker in Bangladesh. The program, known as Innovation Countdown 2030, set out to "identify, evaluate, and showcase health technologies and interventions with great promise to accelerate progress toward solving the world's most urgent health issues." In October, Dr. Grabowsky, Dr. Sarker, and Doug Jackson, the president and CEO of Project C.U.R.E. in Denver, nominated DiaResQ for one of the 30 or so innovation awards to be announced in the summer of 2015.

* * *

In his July 2014 letter to PanTheryx shareholders, Mark had included a reference to the Bangladesh trial, acknowledging that "it has become apparent that our failure to achieve statistical significance has delayed our ability to finalize some distribution deals and obtain regulatory approvals in certain countries. As a result, we have rethought our entire clinical program."

In the course of discussions with Dr. Reddy's, Alok Sonig had requested that "in order to maximize the marketing impact of our next study," PanTheryx increase the number of patients participating in the study to at least 200. PanTheryx agreed that a successful, larger, and more tightly controlled clinical trial would provide the ultimate vindication for PanTheryx, dispelling the doubts raised by the first trial.

The company scrambled to find facilities and clinicians capable of carrying out a large study in a timely fashion. Doug Jackson facilitated an introduction to Dr. Stephen Berman at the University of Colorado Center for Global Health in Denver. The center's stated mission was "to catalyze equitable partnerships in teaching, research, practice, and service to make innovative and creative advances in the global standard of health." In pursuit of this mission, the center collaborated with partners in underdeveloped countries around the world. Its location, mission, and partnering agenda aligned with PanTheryx's clinical study objectives. After meeting with the company, Dr. Berman agreed to be the principal investigator for the new study.

Dr. Berman is a professor of pediatrics at the University of Colorado School of Medicine and School of Public Health and the director of the Center for Global Health. He is a past president of the American Academy of Pediatrics and has served as special advisor to the World Health Organization and the United States Agency for International Development (USAID). Dr. Berman is also an internationally renowned authority and researcher in the field of pediatric infectious diseases common to underdeveloped countries.

Dr. Berman chose Guatemala for the study. It offered several advantages over Bangladesh, not the least of which was its location. Bangladesh was 12 hours ahead of Colorado and entailed a flight of 30 hours or more from Denver. Guatemala shared the same time zone and was a mere six-hour plane ride away.

Dr. Berman and his team proposed to run two double-blind, placebo-controlled studies: an inpatient study at the Roosevelt Hospital in Guatemala City and an outpatient study at the Center for Human Development Clinic, a six-hour drive west of Guatemala City in the rural village of Trifinio, near the Pacific Ocean. Both clinics were closely affiliated with Dr. Berman and the University of Colorado.

The Berman clinical study would be more expansive than any previous trial sponsored by PanTheryx for DiaResQ. With 600 patients enrolled, the study would involve 10 times the number of subjects in the original trial at icddr,b. In addition, the protocol designed by Dr. Berman and his team would measure not only the speed by which DiaResQ resolved an episode of diarrhea, but also the overall impact the product had on malnutrition and weight gain.

For the first time, the team would assess the economic benefits derived from the product's efficacy. The PanTheryx team believed this data would be particularly valuable in convincing public channels of distribution, including NGOs, to participate in dispensing the product throughout the world.

Most clinical studies conducted by hospitals require approval by an Institutional Review Board, or IRB. The IRB has authority to approve, monitor, modify, or disapprove research projects involving human subjects. According to the FDA, the primary objective of the IRB process is "to ensure protection of the rights and welfare of human subjects of research." The Guatemala study's complexity and multiple venues required approval by three different IRBs, each comprised of a distinct group of clinicians and participants.

The product's unique composition, combined with the fact that the IRB members had never encountered a diarrhea product purporting to act with such speed and efficacy, prolonged scrutiny, debate, and evaluation. Longer than expected deliberations involving approval from the Guatemala Ministry of Health and granting of import permits, also due to the product's unique characteristics, would postpone the beginning of the Guatemala study to early 2015.

13

A Strategic Inflection Point

A strategic inflection point is a time in the life of a business
when its fundamentals are about to change.
—Andy Grove, co-founder and CEO, Intel

As the PanTheryx management team scrambled to launch new
clinical trials in the waning days of 2014, some early investors in the
company voiced frustration with the time elapsed since their original
investments and the recurring delays in bringing the business plan to
fruition. Many smaller investors had held stock in the company for
seven years or more and were reaching out to management and board
members asking how they might sell stock.

As the point person on the board for handling many of these calls,
I did my best to persuade investors, many of whom were friends of
mine, that the company was making tangible progress and that their
patience would be rewarded. In doing so, of course, I was aware that

my personal credibility was also being tested. More troubling, I also knew management was contemplating a bold change in strategy that would summon even greater shareholder forbearance.

Among the issues confronting the management team, a looming dilemma began to percolate through deliberations about future growth. Although sales of DiaResQ remained trivial relative to the size of the potential market, Mark Braman's visionary instincts focused on the future impact PanTheryx might have on the market for a primary ingredient of DiaResQ—bovine colostrum. The issue triggered a series of management discussions focused on various "what if…" scenarios. The inevitable conclusion was unsettling.

Because DiaResQ was designed from the outset to address pediatric diarrhea in the world's poorest countries, maintaining a low price point was imperative. If the PanTheryx sales projections for DiaResQ were to be believed, the resulting surge in demand for colostrum would prompt the cost of colostrum and, in turn, DiaResQ to skyrocket, crushing the company's optimistic projections and scuttling its business plan. In other words, the company stood on the precipice of a tumultuous shift in the market that would be precipitated by the company itself.

Andy Grove, the legendary co-founder and CEO of Intel, wrote that most enterprising companies over time encounter "a strategic inflection point," which he defined as "a time in the life of a business when its fundamentals are about to change." Grove argued that "a strategic inflection point can be deadly when unattended to" but can also create unique opportunities for those adept at recognizing and adapting to change, most notably when the company itself is the impetus for the change.

Forces that radically alter the competitive landscape can impale a company on a strategic inflection point before it can respond and avoid disaster. Grove anticipated the very dilemma facing PanTheryx, suggesting that a company's suppliers might become sufficiently powerful to disrupt the traditional structure of an industry by applying newfound leverage to raise prices. Grove offered an ominous warning regarding suppliers: "Are there a lot of them, so that the business has plenty of choices, or are there few of them, so that they have the business by the throat?"

The two key ingredients of DiaResQ are eggs and bovine colostrum. The availability of eggs never posed a problem: the U.S. alone has over 190 egg-producing companies, with flocks of 75,000 or more laying hens producing over 80 billion eggs each year. In the case of colostrum, on the other hand, the departure from the market of the largest producer, New Zealand-based Fonterra, left the three largest U.S. companies in control of over 80 percent of the bovine colostrum processed for human and animal consumption.

Colostrum is the first premilk secretion produced in the mammary glands of mammals immediately following the birth of an infant. Composed of a complex mixture of antibodies, nutrients, vitamins, minerals, and growth factors that stimulate the newborn's immune system, colostrum has been called "nature's perfect first food." Because colostrum is a relatively recent entry into the world of nutritional supplements, it has not been the subject of extensive scientific research. However, a number of studies suggest that bovine colostrum may be a promising therapeutic platform for a variety of diseases. One study even found that colostrum could be three times more effective than vaccination in preventing flu.

As discussed earlier, with an early boost from colostrum, breastfeeding by humans provides enormous immunological and nutritional benefits to the newborn child, in effect passing the mother's immune system on to the child. The longer the child is breastfed, the greater the benefits.

Bovine colostrum, reputed to contain as much as 40 times the number of immune factors as human colostrum, is a relatively recent addition to the panoply of nutritional health supplements available for human consumption. Although it has been studied for decades for its immunological properties, colostrum was considered a low-value stock food until the 1980s. As more scientific evidence emerged verifying its health benefits, widespread collection and processing of bovine colostrum for the human and animal markets began to flourish.

The collection and production of colostrum entails a sequence of complex, labor-intensive steps. The larger colostrum processors contract with hundreds of geographically dispersed dairy farms to purchase colostrum produced by hundreds of thousands of cows. Fortunately, cows produce significantly more colostrum than their calves require, allowing the excess to be collected and used for other purposes.

Because the mother cow's first day of milking following birth yields the most potent mixture of immune and growth factors, this is the most sought-after grade of colostrum. After the calves consume roughly 25 percent, the remainder is frozen at the dairy site. The processor then collects the frozen raw colostrum in refrigerated trucks and transfers it to regional warehouses and eventually to a processing plant where it is subjected to scrupulous quality control procedures, pasteurized, and dried into a yellow powder.

An in-depth analysis of the market by PanTheryx revealed there were very few suppliers who could meet the PanTheryx demand for the highest-quality colostrum, and that the complex supply chain requirements created massive barriers for new processors to enter the business. Unless the company acted to address the shifting landscape before the demand for DiaResQ burgeoned, a mere handful of suppliers would literally, echoing Grove's admonition, "have the business by the throat."

Management concluded the most effective strategy to avoid this outcome would be to vertically integrate, acquiring one or more colostrum producers and thereby ensuring a steady, low-cost supply of DiaResQ's key ingredient. On the other hand, for a company with virtually no revenue, in the midst of crucial clinical trials evaluating the efficacy of its product, pursuing an acquisition strategy could be deemed by its stakeholders as untimely if not fundamentally reckless. The team faced the daunting task of convincing the board and the shareholders not only that a vertical integration strategy would benefit the company long-term but also that major new financing to fund the strategy could be accomplished on terms acceptable to the existing investors.

The benefits to PanTheryx of acquiring one or more high-quality colostrum suppliers were compelling. In addition to being a key ingredient in DiaResQ, colostrum was a strategic component of the company's technology platform, most notably in the value of its intellectual property and the development of future product line extensions. Owning its own supplier, of course, would eliminate the mark-up otherwise paid to an outside supplier, thereby substantially increasing PanTheryx's profit margins.

Since colostrum suppliers typically enjoyed robust profit margins, the proposed acquisitions would further accelerate PanTheryx's path to profitability. Ultimately, by curtailing the risk of suppliers gouging the company, the move would almost certainly enhance the company's valuation as reflected in a sale of the business or a public offering of its stock.

During the last quarter of 2014, before pitching potential investors and existing shareholders on the merits of the idea, the PanTheryx team conducted an exhaustive analysis of the U.S. colostrum market and its major players. All of the leading colostrum suppliers were privately held, many having been owned and managed by the same family for decades. As a result, detailed financial information about the companies was not publicly available. The team scrutinized industry data and news reports and held off-the-record conversations to narrow the field to a small set of candidates.

The most appealing acquisition candidate was Phoenix-based APS BioGroup, the world's largest supplier of colostrum for human health products. As mentioned earlier, shortly after joining PanTheryx in 2011, Braman had mused about buying APS at some point. By 2014, the business relationship between the two companies had blossomed. APS supplied colostrum to PanTheryx and also manufactured finished goods for the company in its state-of-the-art Arizona plant. One aspect of the relationship had not changed since 2011: PanTheryx's revenue remained minuscule compared to that of APS BioGroup.

To maintain the utmost confidentiality during the acquisition process, a code name was assigned to the project for internal communications. After a whimsical contest among the company's 14 employees, "Project Sapphire" was selected. In announcing the contest winner, it was noted that "the sapphire stone represents strong communication, insight, intuition and the ability to see into the future," all attributes that "will help make this project thrive."

In September 2014, Mark launched Project Sapphire by visiting with Bob Davies, the chief executive officer of APS, to broach the concept of combining the two companies. Davies, who had contemplated retirement, was receptive to further discussions. However, Davies cautioned that, to move forward, he would want to solicit input from his two partners. The two companies agreed to explore a possible acquisition. An arduous, complex, and protracted negotiation, one that would challenge the patience and conviction of participants on both sides of the table, began.

***

As the PanTheryx team continued working to complete the angel round of financing, with its daunting $10 million goal, it was clear the acquisition of a colostrum supplier would require a considerably larger financial war chest. The creation of that war chest would be another important juncture in the history of PanTheryx—a shift from the traditionally clubby, unstructured sphere of angel funding to the more formal and onerous world of private equity.

My experience with such transitions suggests that piloting the company through this process would be like transforming a pickup basketball team into an NBA franchise in a matter of weeks. Such a shift is a jarring passage for any early-stage company and its investors—the angels confronting the peril of being ignored personally and crushed financially; the management shouldering the challenge of mutating the company into a fully adult enterprise. The team would now be tasked with satisfying relentless due diligence demands, generating squeaky clean audited financial statements, and implementing structural and governance protocols more akin to those of a public company.

Notwithstanding the potential impediments, the PanTheryx management team and board agreed to move forward with the vertical integration strategy. While approaching a broad spectrum of potential funding sources, Mark connected with Anthony Zolezzi, an environmental and nutritional foods consultant who had worked with Mark on other companies in the past. Anthony suggested Mark meet with Craig Cogut at Pegasus Capital Advisors, a private equity firm based in New York City.

As a PanTheryx board member and investor, my head burst with warning alarms at the thought of a private equity firm investing in (or plundering) "our" company. From my viewpoint as an angel investor, private equity firms conjured visions of heavy-handed predators wresting control of a company away from the early investors and then mercilessly piling on debt, firing employees, and selling off the remains at the earliest opportunity. In other words, my initial reaction to the idea of working with a typical private equity firm was that it would be anathema to a company and its investors dedicated to conquering the world's second leading killer of young children. As we would soon learn, Pegasus was no ordinary private equity firm.

After attending Harvard law school, followed by several years in investment banking and private equity, Craig Cogut struck out on his own in 1996 to launch Pegasus as an innovative, mission-driven private equity firm seeking to "make money by solving fundamental needs of societies" around the world. Reciting his underlying rationale to me several years later, Craig described his disenchantment with the prototypical private equity focus on making money by repeatedly closing humdrum transactions. He and his team had found a "whole new set of motivations and excitement" in helping build companies with the potential to make a difference to underserved people in the world—without sacrificing financial returns.

Rather than employing financial engineering to overleverage a company with debt and reduce overhead, Pegasus focuses on "sustainability" with a "deep commitment to creating fundamental value and lasting impact for companies addressing resource scarcity," including energy, food, and water, as well as improving health and wellness. To my way of thinking, the Pegasus mission statement harmoniously echoes the Leather Apron Club's credo of "doing well by doing good."

Learning that Mark Braman was looking for a sizable round of private equity for PanTheryx, Anthony Zolezzi, in his role as an operating advisor to Pegasus, saw a suitable match. Anthony regaled Craig with the PanTheryx story: an "amazing management team" using a nutritional food product to solve a worldwide health crisis. Remembering the initial discussion, Craig told me his response was,

"Anthony, you have got to be kidding me. If it was that easy, someone would already have done it."

Shortly after his initial meeting with APS in mid-September, Mark scheduled what he expected to be a brief introductory meeting with Cogut at Pegasus' New York offices. As Mark and Scott Hyman presented an overview of the PanTheryx story, Craig interrupted to notify his assistant to cancel the next two meetings on his calendar. He then sent an associate to a third. Despite having had a "great meeting" with Mark in New York—and aware of the scope of the problem from his years of international travel—Craig remained skeptical. When I asked him what took him from skeptic to believer, his response touched a familiar chord: "Until you use the product, you can't become a total believer." Craig's epiphany occurred on a 10-hour flight from Uganda, when one dose of DiaResQ ended a potentially miserable bout of diarrhea acquired from tainted ice cubes served on the plane.

After some preliminary jousting, as the two sides sparred over the basic structure for a transaction, by mid-November Pegasus had presented the company with a preliminary term sheet outlining a potential investment of over $50 million. Negotiations continued through the end of the year as other Pegasus partners and advisors started using the product only to immediately become, in Craig's words, "total champions of the company."

The due diligence process began with Pegasus submitting hundreds of detailed questions about the company, its intellectual property, contracts, financials, suppliers, partners, and more. Scott Hyman assumed the role of point person to coordinate timely responses to these requests. By late January, Pegasus and PanTheryx reached agreement on a final term sheet for the financing of the vertical integration strategy. Simultaneously, PanTheryx had begun submitting its own due diligence shopping list to APS as it kicked off acquisition discussions.

Under a cobalt-blue Colorado sky in early January 2015, my wife, Susan, and I joined 11 other members of the Leather Apron Club for lunch at an investor's house on the mountainside overlooking Vail Village. As eager skiers scurried toward the slopes below, Mark, George, and Scott spelled out the new vertical integration strategy, highlighting the progressing discussions with Pegasus and APS.

Despite the size of the proposed financing, the team encountered virtually no pushback regarding the inevitable dilution likely to be suffered by the angel investors. Of course, management would experience the same dilution in its ownership. In other words, the investors were aligned with management, recognizing the proposal would result in their owning a smaller piece of a much larger, faster-growing company, more than offsetting the initial dilution—*if* the strategy worked.

Most of the group agreed with the strategic shift in the company's vision, but a few members voiced concern: How, they wondered, could we justify buying a company with substantial revenue when we had yet to prove our own revenue model? More pressingly, how would we manage more than a hundred employees when we'd never had more than a handful? Did we have the breadth and depth of management needed to operate a much larger, more complex enterprise?

The team continued the dialogue with investors over the following weeks, acknowledging that their questions were reasonable but emphasizing that the risks were tractable and outweighed by the upside opportunities. Meanwhile, cordial discussions with APS BioGroup continued, though progress toward an actual agreement was labored and tentative. Having completed many acquisitions during their Pfizer days, the process was familiar to the PanTheryx team. But, as Mark told me, "it's much harder to buy something that's not for sale."

In May 2015, PanTheryx quietly reached out to the second-largest domestic colostrum producer—La Belle, Inc. La Belle traced its origin to the early 1980s, when members of the Wiebe family, leading poultry famers in Bellingham, Washington, for several decades, began producing bovine colostrum. Now with a third generation of the Wiebe family at the helm, the company was recognized as a high-quality producer of colostrum for both animal and human consumption, with manufacturing facilities in Bellingham and Ripon, California.

For founders and family members who had spent years, even decades, creating, nurturing, and growing La Belle into a flourishing enterprise, relinquishing ownership would be as wrenching as surrendering a child. Having sold their own early-stage companies in the past, Mark and other members of PanTheryx management were acutely aware of the emotional and financial angst the process arouses. Negotiations with APS and La Belle would require patience, respect, and empathy entwined with a compelling narrative of accelerated growth and prosperity accruing to all parties.

As the negotiations dragged on through 2015, momentum at PanTheryx on other fronts appeared to quicken. Enrollment of patients in the clinical trials underway in Guatemala was proceeding apace. Results were expected by year's end. In June, the company executed closing documents for the Pegasus financing, a crucial step toward accomplishing the vertical integration strategy approved earlier in the year. The transaction provided PanTheryx with over $50 million to pursue acquisitions, expand worldwide marketing and partnering opportunities, and lay the groundwork for launching DiaResQ in the United States market.

***

Indeed, PanTheryx was transitioning to a worldwide presence—a remarkable achievement for a relatively new outfit with just over a dozen employees. The company now had patents on DiaResQ in China, Bangladesh, Pakistan, South Africa, and Yemen, with many more underway in other countries. Distribution partnerships were in place with pharmaceutical companies in Malaysia, Indonesia, and the Philippines, to be followed by similar pacts in Singapore, Brunei, Cambodia, Nigeria, and South America. Importantly, the relationship with Dr. Reddy's had expanded from India and Nepal to include distribution in 11 other countries in Asia, South America, and the Russian Commonwealth with the potential to add up to an additional 15 countries in the near term.

***

Following the Millennium Summit in 2000, the United Nations had established Millennium Development Goals to catalyze a new global focus on ending preventable maternal and child deaths. The goals were subsequently updated with health targets to be achieved by 2030 as outlined in the United Nations Sustainable Development Goals. Global nonprofit PATH sought ideas from experts, innovators, and developers worldwide for health solutions with the potential to accelerate the world's progress toward these targets.

In July 2015, the inaugural report of the Innovation Countdown 2030 selected DiaResQ as one of 30 lifesaving innovations "with great promise to accelerate progress toward solving the world's most urgent health issues" over the next 15 years.

Over 500 innovations from around the world were nominated for the awards. The 30 winners were selected by a worldwide panel of independent health experts. In addition to PATH, the initiative was supported by the Bill and Melinda Gates Foundation and USAID.

The report cited DiaResQ as a new treatment with the "promise to reduce the burden of severe diarrhea" by supplementing the use of oral rehydration solutions and providing nutrients for intestinal repair. It also emphasized that the product "has the advantage of being given orally only once a day," concluding that it "will help children in developing countries have a better chance at recovery." In a celebratory letter announcing the award to the company's shareholders, Mark Braman highlighted the award's validation of the team's long-held belief that DiaResQ offered "the potential to greatly improve the well-being and quality of life of millions of children and their families worldwide."

Despite the expanding relationship with Dr. Reddy's, the regulatory muddle in India continued to bedevil management's efforts to launch DiaResQ in the country where it was most needed. But in mid-summer, good news arrived—this time from the Indian courts. As described earlier, when PanTheryx prepared to enter the Indian market in 2011, FSSAI, the India food and drug regulatory body, inexplicably proclaimed that manufacturers of food-based products must seek pre-market approval from the agency before the products could be sold in India. PanTheryx argued that this exceeded FSSAI's authority. In mid-2014, the courts affirmed this position. Scott Hyman was cautiously optimistic but noted that "the table has basically been reset to where things stood in January 2012 before the premarket-approval requirement was imposed."

Unwilling to surrender its authority, FSSAI appealed the case to India's Supreme Court while issuing new regulations dealing with food product approvals. To the relief of PanTheryx and Dr. Reddy's, in August 2015 the Supreme Court denied the appeal, rendering the lower court decision conclusive. Although the position taken by the company in 2011 had been vindicated, the product's entry into the India market had been delayed by four years, likely costing many lives and untold misery for millions of families.

***

For several months, Mark Braman had contemplated augmenting the management team with a respected authority in disease prevention and child health. When Dr. Mark Grabowsky indicated he would step down as the chief operating officer of the UN Millennium Development Goals program, Braman leapt at the chance to hire him. Grabowsky joined PanTheryx as vice president of public initiatives, where he would oversee all future clinical trials.

Mark Grabowsky grew up in a military family of eight children, moving up and down the east coast every two years. In the late 1970s, he entered the Peace Corps, where he worked as a high school teacher in rural Kenya, near Lake Victoria. Before long, he realized that his students, most of whom were coping with ordeals like malaria, diarrhea, and early pregnancies, "were just too sick to learn." The experience was transformative, convincing Mark to pursue a career in public health.

Grabowsky recalls medical school as the place where he identified his "ethical touchstone": he would focus on how he could "do the most good for the most people." In the late 1980s, as he prepared to enter the world health-care arena, polio, measles, and malaria were among the most daunting unresolved health challenges facing the underdeveloped world. Over the next 25 years, in leadership positions with the World Health Organization, Centers for Disease Control and Prevention, National Institutes of Health, and the American Red Cross, Mark played a crucial role in helping to eradicate or minimize the impact of these diseases.

In the 1990s, Grabowsky traveled the world establishing foundational programs to eliminate polio. By 2000, he was leading a global Measles Initiative to vaccinate children. Over five years, worldwide measles deaths declined 90 percent, from 500,000 each year to 50,000.

When I spoke to him in 2017, Mark proudly reported that three years earlier the program had vaccinated its one-*billionth* child.

For Mark, the next unaddressed problem was malaria, a mosquito-borne disease caused by a parasite. Mark helped launch the Alliance for Malaria Prevention to provide insecticide-treated bed nets to families in underdeveloped countries. Mark reported to me that two years ago the campaign delivered its one-billionth bed net, and that malaria had declined by 60 percent.

When I asked Mark what had attracted him to PanTheryx, he told me that diarrhea is the "last great unsolved global health problem." It represented an untapped opportunity to "do the greatest good for the greatest number of people." His research revealed that 80 percent of diarrhea deaths worldwide could not be addressed with currently available treatments like ORS and zinc. He noted that 20 percent of childhood deaths from diarrhea occur in the first two weeks after birth. For another 80 percent of children who die from diarrhea, the death occurs in the first two years of life. In other words, an early diarrhea episode is a marker for early death. It was clear that "the risk of death decreases with every additional month the child survives."

As he learned more about PanTheryx, Mark realized that DiaResQ was "the first solution for diarrhea that had the promise of both stopping the course of the infection and repairing the gut." In summarizing the appeal of the PanTheryx product, Mark's comments echoed Tim Starzl's discussions with me seven years earlier: "It replicates breastfeeding by creating a passive immunity that can be effectively and immediately delivered to the child. The fact that this result can be provided cheaply in the form of a food product is groundbreaking."

14

Statistically Significant Efficacy

It's not wanting to win that makes you a winner; it's refusing to fail.

—Peyton Manning

Going into 2016, the PanTheryx management team and board expressed cautious optimism about the anticipated results from the Guatemala study. As the University of Colorado team in Guatemala continued to enroll new patients in Guatemala City and Trifinio, the importance of a favorable outcome to the future of PanTheryx preoccupied the company.

Attending another early January meeting of the Leather Apron Club at my house in the Vail valley, PanTheryx management discussed sanguine reports detailing the retail launch of DiaResQ in the United States, on the Internet, and in the international travelers' market. In contrast to the skeptical dialogue a year earlier, solid progress in acquisition discussions with two colostrum companies appeared to energize the investor group.

After years of lingering skepticism about the credibility of the 2010–2011 field trials of DiaResQ in India, the 2016 clinical trials in Guatemala City rewarded PanTheryx with the vindication that had eluded it for so long. In July 2016, Dr. James Gaensbauer and Dr. Stephen Berman at the Colorado School of Public Health and the University of Colorado School of Medicine reported the first statistically significant clinical proof of the efficacy of DiaResQ against its targeted pathogens in a randomized, double-blind, placebo-controlled study. In December 2017, the researchers revealed the detailed results of the trials in a peer-reviewed article published in the prestigious *British Medical Journal.*

From the outset, the researchers identified Guatemala as an exceedingly challenging environment for a clinical trial based on the country's unexpectedly high and diverse number of pathogens per patient. In the United States, the average diarrhea patient has one diarrhea-causing pathogen. By comparison, patients in the urban Guatemala setting had an average of nearly three. Patients in the rural setting had an astonishing average of nearly five pathogens. Simply stated, these kids were extraordinarily sick.

Over 300 children, ages 6 to 35 months, participated in the study between the two clinics. Each patient was given one dose of DiaResQ per day for three consecutive days. In addition to analyzing stool samples at the beginning of the trial, the researchers used polymerase chain reaction (PCR) to analyze patient stool samples 30 days after the trial began. By design, DiaResQ specifically targeted four of the most common causes of diarrhea worldwide: rotavirus, enterotoxigenic *Escherichia coli* (ETEC), Shiga toxin-producing *E. coli* (STEC), and salmonella (directly targeted). It also has cross-reactivity against two other pathogens: *Shigella*/enteroinvasive *E. coli* (EIEC) and norovirus (indirectly targeted). The study confirmed that in patients in the urban setting with at least one of the targeted pathogens, DiaResQ demonstrated "statistically significant efficacy," reducing the duration of the diarrheal episode by an average of 12 hours.

For these patients, the acute diarrhea is totally resolved at the end of day one in 56 percent of patients, at the end of day two in 88 percent of patients, and at the end of day three in 96 percent of patients. The product was also "found to be very safe." The results at the end of two days were so impressive the doctors speculated that perhaps only two days of treatment with DiaResQ are sufficient to cure the average patient.

Acute pediatric diarrhea episodes in underdeveloped countries frequently last for days or even weeks. The longer the episode, the greater the likelihood of permanent malnutrition, stunting, and eventually death. Until the Guatemala study of DiaResQ, no other intervention had been proven to significantly shorten this horrendous cycle. Equally impressive, no single therapeutic product had been shown to have an immunological effect on the most common diarrhea-causing viruses, bacteria, and protozoa simultaneously. The Guatemala study confirmed that DiaResQ represented a momentous breakthrough in the centuries-old search for an effective cure for diarrhea. It also revealed other fascinating benefits of DiaResQ and suggested several exciting areas for additional research.

Beyond demonstrating efficacy against the directly and indirectly targeted diarrhea-causing pathogens, DiaResQ showed statistically significant results with *C. diff*, a tenacious bacterial infection often affecting people taking antibiotics, and *Cryptosporidium* (Crypto), a microscopic parasite commonly found in contaminated water supplies.

In view of the broad-spectrum capability of the product and its efficacy against targeted pathogens, the researchers and PanTheryx management envision the technology underlying DiaResQ as a therapeutic platform capable of targeting an array of other specific pathogens by region or addressing specific pathogens associated with distinct disease outbreaks. The clinicians also suggested the potential use of DiaResQ as a preventive treatment in areas experiencing epidemic outbreaks or for people traveling to areas where the local environment placed them at high risk of acquiring infectious diarrhea. As discussed earlier, antibiotics are often overprescribed in treating pediatric diarrhea even though they are only effective, if at all, in cases caused by bacteria alone. The researchers noted that the ability to target diarrhea caused by specific pathogens "suggest the tantalising possibility" that DiaResQ could replace treatment with antibiotics in some cases.

Since their introduction over 70 years ago, antibiotics have become the bulwark of our defense against infectious disease worldwide. However, the overuse of antibiotics has resulted in the evolution of antibiotic-resistant "superbugs." The Centers for Disease Control and Prevention estimates that in the United States alone at least two million people become infected every year with bacteria that are resistant to antibiotics, causing more than 23,000 deaths. The indiscriminate use of antibiotics in children with infectious diarrhea is especially worrisome because it launches the resistance process so early in life. Replacing antibiotics used for pediatric diarrhea with a low-cost, broad-spectrum intervention like DiaResQ would benefit the long-term health of children throughout the world.

The findings offered by the researchers who conducted the Guatemala clinical trials mirrored the due diligence discussion I'd had with Dr. Peter Nash in 2010. Dr. Nash had suggested Tim's invention might be a viable alternative to antibiotics in treating not only pediatric diarrhea but also cholera, dysentery, *C. diff*, clostridium, and other diseases. Dr. Nash had also predicted that the product might be effective as a prophylactic, used to prevent the occurrence of the diarrhea episode altogether. Once again, the revolutionary solution invented by Tim seven years earlier was living up to expectations.

Patients in the rural arm of the Guatemala study did not fare as well as those in Guatemala City. The rural study area suffers from severe flooding during the rainy season and almost no treated drinking water or sanitary treatment of human waste. As a result, the children are vastly undernourished and carry an average of five or more diarrhea-causing pathogens, many of which were never envisioned as targets for DiaResQ. Indeed, further study has suggested that this population may have the highest pathogen load per stool of any country ever surveyed, far exceeding that of any other part of the world. In this rural population, the product fails to show significant efficacy. Patients are so sick and malnourished that the positive effects of DiaResQ are overwhelmed by the sheer number of pathogens they harbor. This condition epitomizes a rapidly emerging field of study known as "environmental enteropathy," in which the permeability and bacterial resistance of the walls of the intestines are severely compromised by repeated infections and malnutrition. Enteropathy is a primary cause of stunting.

Based on these findings, the company launched a program to study the potential for daily doses of DiaResQ administered over extended periods to curtail or prevent enteropathy by a combination of infection control and nutritional intervention. Additional studies being considered involve the use of DiaResQ as a supplement for infants during the period of weaning from breastfeeding, in effect continuing the nutritional and infection control benefits of mother's milk for the child.

Even with the disappointing aspects of the rural arm of the study, the findings from Guatemala ultimately verified Tim's early hypothesis that the product resolves a "broad spectrum" of diarrheal pathogens. The results are a ringing tribute to Tim and Bimla Starzl's early ingenuity and determination, relying, in Tim's words, on a "garage sale approach" with meager resources, in a hostile environment, on the opposite side of the globe.

When I saw the results myself, I couldn't help but think back, with some satisfaction, to the renowned professor of immunology who called the product "snake oil" and described the first trial in India as "a joke" and "pathetic" in an early due diligence call. As Mark Braman, George Stagnitti, and Scott Hyman proclaimed for years: "We know it works. We just have to convince the rest of the world we're right."

***

More than two years before the Guatemala trial results were announced, PanTheryx management conceded that regulatory delays and inconclusive clinical trial results had coalesced to postpone the revenue projected in its business plan. Scanning the market for rapid entry points, the proximity and familiarity of the United States market for adult and pediatric diarrhea solutions offered an enticing target far too large to ignore.

Mark Braman had no interest in tampering with the company's long-term vision, but he realized that circumstances required a midcourse adjustment (Mark later called it a pivot) in marketing priorities. To that end, the team crafted a strategy to accelerate the U.S. market entry for DiaResQ, positioning it as "a new and innovative breakthrough product that redefines the diarrhea remedy space for the first time in over forty-five years."

The PanTheryx product launch strategy identified three distinct consumer segments worth exploring: travelers, children, and adults. The three leading over-the-counter products for adults at the time generated $350 million in retail sales each year. None of these addressed the root cause of the ailment, and no retail solution for pediatric diarrhea existed at all. But travelers quickly became the primary focus for the U.S. market entry. With total expenditures of $6.6 trillion, tourism is the world's third-largest industry (behind only oil and gas and the military). At least 50 million people travel to underdeveloped countries each year, and 30 to 40 percent of all travelers experience travelers' diarrhea, making it the most common illness affecting international travelers. Each year, 10 million Americans traveling internationally come down with diarrhea.

Based on years of anecdotal experience as well as successful trials in underdeveloped countries, management felt confident DiaResQ is ideal for addressing intestinal issues facing foreign travelers. The Guatemala trial also confirmed that DiaResQ is effective in treating the pathogens most commonly associated with travelers' diarrhea. Because diarrhea is so disruptive and costly to both business and pleasure travel, a simple solution like DiaResQ would be considered a bargain at almost any price.

In 2015, PanTheryx partnered with Passport Health, the largest provider of travel medicine and vaccination services in the United States. Over the next two years, Passport Health rolled out DiaResQ throughout its 250 clinic locations in the United States, calling it the cornerstone of their traveler's diarrhea standard of care: "DiaResQ is the traveler's diarrhea product of choice and a must-have for international travel."

In another emphatic endorsement, returning Passport Health customers waxed enthusiastic about the effectiveness of DiaResQ. In fall 2016, Passport Health reported to the annual meeting of the American Society of Tropical Medicine & Hygiene (ASTMH) that its clinics were experiencing an over 42 percent reduction in antibiotic sales as customers found that DiaResQ worked more effectively than antibiotics. By spring 2017, DiaResQ had become one of Passport Health's best-selling products.

Early success in the travel market inspired an aggressive push into consumer retail and online marketing as well. Thanks to the Pegasus funding, the company had sufficient operating capital to begin the long-delayed build-out of the management team, launching executive searches for sales and marketing leadership.

Brian Budeselich joined the company as vice president of sales, bringing 18 years of consumer package sales experience focused on health and wellness products. Joining the company as vice president of marketing, Jessica Teilborg had spent over 15 years in strategic marketing in the consumer-packaged goods industry with extensive expertise in e-commerce, digital media, and social networking solutions.

In 2016, the company launched sales of DiaResQ on Amazon.com, accompanied by an aggressive social media campaign. For the travelers' market, humorous ads on sites like Facebook were particularly effective. One shows a young couple in an airport with the caption, "Check your Baggage, Not Your Trousers. DiaResQ, almost as vital as your passport." Another features an older couple with a cruise ship in the background and the caption: "Don't Let the Poop-Deck Ruin Your Cruise. DiaResQ, the best travel insurance you can buy."

By early 2017, PanTheryx was in discussions with over 100 retail customers, drug wholesalers, and regional and national grocery accounts. By the end of the year, DiaResQ was on the shelves of thousands of retail stores throughout the United States.

***

Increasing international sales combined with a successful rollout of DiaResQ in the United States heightened management's eagerness to lock down a reliable source of colostrum. Through much of 2015 and 2016, prolonged acquisition negotiations continued with two leading colostrum manufacturers—APS and La Belle. As anticipated, discussions were cordial but revealed disparities between the parties over timing, valuations, future management, and many other issues both significant and surprisingly trivial—depending on your perspective. Thankfully, all parties persevered: the acquisition by PanTheryx of La Belle closed in July 2016 followed by the acquisition of APS BioGroup in late December of that year.

Mark Braman reported to shareholders that PanTheryx was now "the premier colostrum producer in the world, with over a thousand dairies and over a million cows in our supply network." In just over a year, PanTheryx had grown from 15 employees and tens of thousands of dollars in revenue to 150 employees and tens of millions in revenue.

The company approached the end of 2017 with a fresh array of management initiatives: expanding international and domestic sales, clearance of remaining regulatory hurdles in dozens of countries, integration of two manufacturing operations, consummation of a growing portfolio of international distribution partnerships, the planning of additional clinical trials, and diversification of its product offerings. The days of nurturing a struggling startup were at long last relegated to nostalgic memories. The beguiling prospect of forging a mature, profitable, world-class company was now at hand.

15

A Medical Nutrition Company

All disease starts in the gut.
                            —Hippocrates

This book chronicles the journey of PanTheryx through the end of 2017, exactly seven years after the Leather Apron Club's first investment in Tim and Bimla Starzl's fledgling startup. The vision of the founders and the early investors to conquer a neglected disease with a simple solution is now within reach.

As I finish writing this, PanTheryx is launching DiaResQ in over 40 countries around the globe through its numerous international partners; enjoys patents issued or approved in dozens of countries and regions including the United States, the European Union, China, Pakistan, and South Africa; has diversified into the world's largest producer of bovine colostrum; and is conducting a variety of clinical trials involving technological advances in Guatemala, Russia, Pakistan, Bangladesh, and the Netherlands.

As the management team shifts into overdrive, the future for PanTheryx looks promising indeed. That future is likely to be defined largely by the company's ability to master two enormous opportunities: comprehending and exploiting the mysteries of the human microbiome and assuring that its revolutionary product reaches the neediest families in the places that are hardest to reach.

**

From 2008 through 2012, Tim Starzl wrote several short manuscripts explaining the PanTheryx technology platform using scholarly research into the science underlying his invention. Although these papers are replete with references to microorganisms, pathogens, antibodies, and viruses, collectively known as microbes, Tim does not use terminology widely employed today to describe the universe in which these invisible creatures reside.

Based on the success of the Human Genome Project, scientists at the National Institutes of Health and elsewhere envisioned a project of equally monumental significance to comprehend the massive assemblage of microbes that live in and on the human body. In 2008 the National Institutes of Health announced the launch of the Human Microbiome Project to catalog and describe these microbes.

New DNA genomic sequencing techniques dramatically accelerated the mapping of the human genome by enabling the automation of painstaking work that had formerly required years of effort. The availability of this efficient technology became a driver for the launch of the Human Microbiome Project and hastened it toward completion.

When the results of the first phase of the Human Microbiome Project were announced in 2012, it was hailed as the beginning of a new frontier in science and medicine. In 2016, a leading biologist declared that we now realize "microbes are the centre of the universe" and that this is "the most significant revolution in biology since Darwin." Another expert described developments in understanding the human microbiome that are emerging from the project as the beginning of a "revolution in science."

Since the first investment in PanTheryx by the Leather Apron Club, human microbiome research has mushroomed into an exciting field of scientific inquiry. A PubMed search for mentions of "microbiome" in research papers turns up about 450 in 2007, the year of PanTheryx's founding. In 2016, the number of mentions in the scientific literature was over 8,300. At the end of 2017, new mentions of "microbiome" are appearing at the rate of about 750 a week.

Every year, the Cleveland Clinic announces the top 10 medical innovations that have the potential to transform health care in the forthcoming year. In its list for 2017, the number-one innovation is "using the microbiome to prevent, diagnose, and treat disease." In early 2017, Merriam-Webster added "microbiome" to the English dictionary.

The average human gut contains over 100 trillion microbes, 10 times the number of cells in the entire body. Most of these microbes are bacteria residing in the small and large intestines, where DiaResQ performs its magic. Contrary to what most of us were taught growing up, over 99 percent of these microbial bacteria are beneficial— indeed, crucial—to our health and well-being. Only a small fraction of human microbes cause disease.

As the human microbiome steadily gained stature in the scientific community, researchers and medical experts began to call it an "essential organ," and "the forgotten organ, the unseen organ." When this organ fails to maintain the appropriate balance of each of the hundreds of species of microbes in the gut, a wide range of diseases and adverse conditions can follow. For example, when pathogens find their way to the gut, harmful imbalance in the composition of the gut microbiome may ensue (known as "dysbiosis"), provoking or contributing to disease. Dysbiosis is also linked to a variety of clinical conditions including obesity, autoimmune diseases, cancer, depression, diabetes, and allergies.

As we have discussed, certain pathogens ingested with tainted water or food make their way to the intestinal tract and cause diarrhea. The Human Microbiome Project reveals that diarrhea is a form of dysbiosis involving damage to the walls of the intestine combined with an imbalance of nutritional components and immune factors in the gut microbiome. When the gut is in its normal harmonious balance, its beneficial microbes organize to effectively fight off invading pathogens, a process known as "colonization resistance." When the microbiome is unbalanced, however, this natural resistance can collapse, allowing the pathogens to flourish. This is essentially what happens when a malnourished child or one with a compromised immune system ingests pathogen-riddled food or water.

Evidence generated on the heels of the Human Microbiome Project confirms the overuse of antibiotics as a major cause of dysbiosis. Antibiotics indiscriminately attack and kill many different types of bacteria, including the good microbes essential to maintaining gut health. Repeated or even occasional use of antibiotics inflicts potentially lasting damage to the normal healthy balance of microbiota in the human microbiome. The effect, especially in children, can be devastating, altering the function of the immune system, damaging the protective cellular layer in the walls of the intestine, and triggering inflammation in the intestinal tract. This explains why all respected world health organizations discourage the use of antibiotics in treating pediatric diarrhea except in a rare subset of extreme cases.

DiaResQ not only offers an alternative to antibiotics for treating pediatric diarrhea, thereby reducing the likelihood of antibiotic resistance, but it also markedly reduces the negative effects inflicted on the microbiome by the use of antibiotics. DiaResQ in essence loans the consumer an immune system to repel and destroy the invading pathogens while restoring the normal balance to the gut microbiome, reducing inflammation, reestablishing normal immune function, and repairing the damage to the lining of the intestine.

In order for DiaResQ to reach the imbalanced areas of the gut and restore the appropriate balance, it must first pass through the stomach and areas of the small intestine. There, it is marinated in acids and enzymes that would ordinarily dismantle it for digestion into the bloodstream. If that happened, it would prevent the product's unique combination of nutrients and antibodies from reaching the large intestine where the majority of microbes reside.

To address this problem, DiaResQ's technology combines proteins and other factors from eggs and colostrum during the manufacturing process to create a protective matrix around its antibodies and nutritional components. The clinical trials in Guatemala confirm that, like an armored vehicle ferrying troops through a minefield, this protective matrix allows these key components to travel safely through the digestive tract and reach the gut without being degraded or destroyed.

As it passes through the small intestine and enters the large intestine, DiaResQ immediately begins promoting the maintenance and repair of the cells in the tissue lining the intestinal walls. At the same time, it releases proteins and nutrients important in boosting the immune response to the invading pathogens and unleashing antibodies targeted specifically at the known diarrhea-causing pathogens. Finally, these proteins and antibodies bind with the infectious pathogens and flush them out of the gut.

Scientists intrigued with the implications of the microbiome for health and wellness include a cadre of practitioners in a rapidly evolving field known as "synthetic biology." The field is so vast and complex that no widely-accepted definition of the term yet exists. One definition calls it "the application of science, technology, and engineering to facilitate…the modification of genetic materials in living organisms to alter living or non-living materials."

The author of a recent best-selling book about the microbiome discusses ongoing university research projects using synthetic biology to send reengineered microbes into the gut to release antibiotics that kill invasive pathogens. In extolling the implications of this work, the author speculates, "You could give it to children in poor countries, who are at risk of diarrhoeal diseases. You could give it to soldiers who deploy overseas. You could pass it around communities that are in the midst of an epidemic."

Reading this passage, I thought: "That is essentially what DiaResQ does today, without the need for potentially damaging antibiotics." But the contrast between DiaResQ and the therapeutic solutions that might someday emerge from synthetic biology could not be starker. For all of its nascent promise, synthetic biology is a biologic drug development process fraught with complexity. At best, it involves years of research followed by lengthy and expensive FDA-approved clinical trials and clearance through a regulatory maze with no currently defined framework. By comparison, DiaResQ exemplifies the familiar dictum of Occam's razor: in attempting to solve a problem, the simplest solution is generally best.

Several years after the invention of oral rehydration solution in the late 1960s, one of its inventors memorialized the experience and its aftermath in a book, *A Simple Solution*. Forty years passed before another "simple solution" was found.

Like the doctors who improvised ORS in the refugee camps near Bangladesh, Tim's determination to improvise a simple solution was driven by his understanding of the harsh realities of life in impoverished countries. Although the invention is simple in its application and use—an inexpensive powder that can be mixed with any potable liquid and consumed—its effectiveness is grounded in a deep understanding of immunology and therapeutic methodology. An "unlikely intervention," indeed. In words attributed to Albert Einstein, "everything should be made as simple as possible, but no simpler."

Nearing the end of 2017, PanTheryx rebranded as a "medical nutrition company" centered on "nutrition-based interventions to address a wide range of serious GI-related health conditions." The company aims to reimagine the future of global health by becoming the leader at the intersection of nutrition-based therapeutic interventions and the human microbiome.

***

Forty years after the Bangladesh cholera epidemic, another devastating cholera epidemic is ravaging an equally impoverished country, where one in nine children dies before their fifth birthday. This catastrophe, however, is unfolding less than 700 miles off the shores of the United States—in Haiti.

A pernicious worldwide health problem, cholera is an acute diarrheal infection caused by waterborne bacteria prevalent in underdeveloped countries with poor sanitation. Most cases can be resolved with time and the administration of oral rehydration solutions, but in countries like Haiti, where many children are severely malnourished, ORS does not act quickly enough to prevent many from dying.

For over 100 years before 2010, Haiti avoided cholera altogether. Tragically, it was brought to Haiti by United Nations peacekeepers sent to aid the inhabitants following an earthquake in 2010. Intensifying the calamity, Hurricane Matthew struck the country in 2016, reenergizing the epidemic and raising the death toll to over 9,000, making it the largest cholera epidemic in recent history.

The dire situation in Haiti had been confronted firsthand by David Crane, a senior operating executive at Pegasus and former CEO of NRG Energy, a large independent power producer. At NRG, Crane pioneered a strategic shift from fossil fuel to clean energy solutions like solar. In the process, he traveled to Haiti regularly over a five-year period, installing solar power in hospitals, clinics, and schools. Before Crane could fulfill his transformative mission at NRG, his board of directors intervened and fired him.

Although Crane's vision was anathema to the energy industry, it aligned perfectly with Craig Cogut's sustainability mission at Pegasus. In spring 2016, Crane joined the private equity firm and quickly took note of the firm's investment in PanTheryx. When Hurricane Matthew struck Haiti the following fall, Crane called Mark Braman to discuss the possibility of securing DiaResQ to treat cholera victims there. Having already initiated a PanTheryx program to deliver DiaResQ to underserved and low-income populations most susceptible to diarrhea disease, Braman mobilized his team to respond.

Within a few days PanTheryx had shipped 30,000 units of DiaResQ in sealed foil sachets to Crane's house in New Jersey. David purchased the supply at PanTheryx's cost by raising money from a handful of friends. As David later explained to me, transporting the product to clinics in Haiti presented a challenge. With help from friends and family members, he packed the sachets into duffel bags, ferried the bags by plane to Port-au-Prince, and then drove them to the few functioning clinics in Haiti. One of these, Klinik Timoun Nou Yo— Creole for Our Children's Clinic—was in the area hardest hit by the hurricane. It is based in Port-Salut; getting there involved a tortuous five-hour drive from Port-au-Prince over a 110-mile, two-lane road to the southeastern end of the country.

As the clinics reported back, David relayed positive news to the company: DiaResQ "worked well," usually with only one dose, even for children with cholera. A doctor at the Port-Salut clinic added, "We could use a thousand units a month" going forward. Follow-up trips with more duffel bags were hastily arranged.

This effort represented just one aspect of a more expansive humanitarian effort inaugurated by PanTheryx in 2015 called the Equity of Access Initiative (EAI). The management and board of directors of PanTheryx have always been dedicated to fulfilling the mission envisioned by the founders to create an affordable, easy-to-use product that serves the poorest and hardest to reach children in underdeveloped countries. In creating the EAI program, they firmly imbedded this mission at the core of the company's culture. The Leather Apron Club members applauded the initiative for confirming their vision of the company "doing well by doing good."

EAI is funded through charitable donations and in-kind support to EAI partner charities, who then purchase DiaResQ from PanTheryx at a steep discount. In time, a separate EAI charitable organization will be established to receive contributions and manage the program. Under the leadership of Scott Hyman, who gathered intelligence on comparable programs operating around the world, the initiative addresses distribution, education, and accountability.

David Crane and his hastily assembled team performed heroically in ferrying DiaResQ to Haiti in duffel bags. But the Equity of Access Initiative demands a more expansive model. EAI's vision cannot rest on a motto like "Reaching the neediest and hardest to reach children, one duffel bag at a time."

PanTheryx had tested a go-it-alone strategy when it initially entered the market in India in 2010 with an in-house sales force. Before long, however, the team realized the most effective and efficient path for a small company to enter a foreign market is to partner with a local pharmaceutical company with a firmly entrenched regulatory, sales, marketing, and distribution infrastructure. This strategic pivot led to the partnering agreement with Dr. Reddy's and several other well-established companies to distribute DiaResQ in underdeveloped countries throughout the world.

The lesson learned in India is the paradigm for distribution of DiaResQ through the EAI program. To guarantee distribution of DiaResQ to remote areas where it is needed most, EAI partners with nonprofit organizations with well-established delivery channels, inventory management systems, and strong relationships with respected local NGOs. The first of these partnerships was struck with Project C.U.R.E., which provides high-quality donated medical supplies and equipment to resource-limited communities across the globe.

In September 2017, PanTheryx employees joined a volunteer day at Project C.U.R.E. headquarters in Denver, loading over 3,000 units of DiaResQ for shipment to clinics in Guatemala. Later that month, the company worked with Project C.U.R.E. to include 10,000 units of DiaResQ in a cargo container of medical supplies destined for earthquake victims in Mexico City.

A crucial aspect of EAI is the collection of data by community health-care workers documenting each case of diarrhea they encounter, including the patient's age, use of ORS and DiaResQ, dosing, antibiotic use, and hospitalization referral rates. Using this data, EAI can monitor the impact of the program on the communities it serves.

For several decades, providing health and wellness education to impoverished families in undeveloped countries has been an overriding priority of world health organizations and NGOs. A good example is BRAC's work, described earlier, in training mothers across Bangladesh how to use ORT. Another is the work of WHO, UNICEF, and other organizations to teach water, sanitation, and hygiene (WASH) in health-care facilities around the world. Programs such as these provided a template for training community health-care workers and caregivers where DiaResQ would be distributed through EAI.

Working with Project C.U.R.E., PanTheryx developed an intensive Diarrhea Management Training Program to facilitate the education of local community health-care workers in the prevention, assessment, and treatment of episodes of diarrhea. These trainees then train the local population in the same techniques, using flash cards and games to illustrate best practices. Teaching simple habits for hand washing, food preparation, and sanitation has markedly reduced the incidence of diarrhea in these poor communities.

EAI also teaches community health-care workers and, in turn, local families, how to recognize and treat the earliest signs of diarrhea, such as dehydration. The course focuses on administration of the current standard of care (oral rehydration solutions and zinc) as well as the proper treatment regimen with DiaResQ. By the end of 2017, PanTheryx had partnered with Project C.U.R.E. to offer diarrhea training programs throughout Mexico and Guatemala. The company also launched fundraising efforts to create similar programs in Pakistan, India, and other countries that need it. The company's quest to assure DiaResQ reached the neediest families in the most remote corners of the world has just begun.

***

As I look back on the odyssey of PanTheryx since 2010, one of my many discussions with Bimla Starzl sums up the company's remarkable progress. Earlier, I described one of the first field trials Bimla led at the clinic run by Dr. Kaushik out of a drab clinic in an impoverished neighborhood of Meerut, India. Noticing children draped on discarded truck tires in the sweltering sun while awaiting treatment, Bimla had placed the sickest in her air-conditioned rental car to cool off.

"I can only do so much, for a very few children, under those circumstances," she told me. "So many of these children were not going to get much better." Pondering the prospect of seeing these depleted children overcome despair and recover, Bimla continued: "Bringing DiaResQ to this kind of environment creates an almost unimaginable benefit for these children; when we finally get this product introduced throughout the world, I can only imagine how big an impact it is going to make on so many lives."

Today, six years later, PanTheryx is positioned to fulfill Bimla's dream, improving the lives of millions with the Starzls' unlikely intervention.

Acknowledgements

Ernest Hemingway, echoing the sentiments of dozens of other writers, said, "Writing, at its best, is a lonely life." As I launched this project five years ago, I failed to grasp the acuity of this insight. The solitude I experienced in writing this book, however, was punctuated and energized by the interactions the project invoked with many wonderfully supportive people.

The story would have no beginning and no end without the details so astutely supplied by Tim and Bimla Starzl. Their detailed storytelling and penetrating observations were crucial in bringing the tale to life.

I congratulate and thank all present and former employees of PanTheryx. Your perseverance through the exhilarating highs and the crushing lows of the PanTheryx journey was an inspiration to me at every turn.

Special thanks to Tom Schultz, Ravi Starzl, Julie Lindemann, Meg Cattell, Matt Braman, Amy Gibbs, Lauren Braman, C. S. Wee, Diane Dustin, Ani Webster, and Arlene Tani. The service and support of board members Dave Cook, Peter Vitulli, and David Cogut have been invaluable and are greatly appreciated.

The management team at PanTheryx took a serious risk by encouraging me to proceed, knowing that I would burden them with interviews and questions, with no certainty that the end product would be deserving of their approval. I thank the many PanTheryx executives who spent hours telling me about themselves and discussing the most minute details of the company. They include Mark Braman, George Stagnitti, Rob Driver, Scott Hyman, Mark Grabowsky, Jessica Teilborg, Jim Hau, Nagendra Rangavajla, and Keith Brenner.

I raise my glass to the angel investors who stepped up to support the company when the risks were enormous and the potential outcome problematic. The early members of the Leather Apron Club were extraordinarily generous, supportive, patient, and loyal. My special thanks to members Jay and Amy Regan, Linda Pancratz, Chris and Anne Wiedenmayer, Gary and Susan Rosenbach, John Conley, Craig Johnson, Steve and Gina Spessard, Merv and Laine Lapin, Mary Baum, Jason and Candace Washing, and Alan and Ann Mintz.

Craig Cogut and David Crane at Pegasus Capital Advisors spared time from their frenetic lives to share vital stories and anecdotes with me. Anthony Zolezzi, also with Pegasus, became a staunch believer, advisor, and cheerleader, always available with warm and thoughtful encouragement when it was most needed. I also wish to thank Dan Arensmeier, Dr. Robert Nash, Brad Feld, and Julie Morgenstern.

For anyone reading this who might be contemplating writing a book for the first time, my advice would be "find a great editor." Based in New York, David Moldawer read an early draft of my book and offered invaluable advice that led me to rethink how I was approaching the endeavor and pointing out numerous flaws in the basic narrative. His editing and comments on my final drafts elevated the manuscript immeasurably. Dave regularly reminds readers of his blog, The Maven Game, that "Writing is Hard." He is most certainly correct; Dave makes it look easy.

My thanks also to Maggie Langrick, Sarah Brohman, and their team at LifeTree Media, Ltd., for providing advice and assistance in publishing this book.

Most important, my family emboldened me every step of the way, refusing to entertain the possibility that I might abandon the project. My son Whit offered praise when I needed it most and spent many hours reading drafts and offering perceptive editing assistance. My son Jason and my daughter Taylor were staunch supporters, always eager for updates and quick to provide reassuring feedback.

After about a year into the project my amazing wife, Susan, sensing that my determination might falter, gave me a small paperweight to set next to my computer as I wrote. On it is inscribed a quote from Winston Churchill: "Never, never, never give up." To Susan: I could never express in words my gratitude for your warmth, your love, and your ceaseless inspiration. I love you very much.

Notes

Introduction

p. 4, *Every day in the developing world...* Centers for Disease Control and
Prevention, "Global Diarrhea Burden," https://www.cdc.gov/
healthywater/global/diarrhea-burden.html.

p. 4, *The risks are not confined to children...* Justin Sonnenburg and Erica
Sonnenburg, *The Good Gut: Taking Control of Your Weight, Your Mood,
and Your Long-Term Health* (New York; Penguin Press, 2015), 164.

p. 4, *The World Health Organization (WHO) defines diarrhea...* http://www.
who.int/topics/diarrhoea/en. The term itself was devised by
Hippocrates around 400 B.C., based on the Greek word *diarroia*,
which means "flowing through." In North America, the disease is
usually spelled "diarrhea," whereas in the United Kingdom and
elsewhere it is often spelled "diarrhoea."

p. 4, *The earliest historical evidence of the disease...* John Kahler, "Acute
Infectious Diarrhea," *Emergency Medicine Reports,* September 30, 2007,
available at https://www.ahcmedia.com/articles/107232-acute-

infectious-diarrhea; M. L. Lim and M. R. Wallace, "Infectious Diarrhea in History," *Infectious Disease Clinics of North America* 18, no. 2 (June 2004): 261–74, http://www.ncbi.nlm.nih.gov/pubmed/15145380; Folke Henschen, *The History of Diseases,* trans. Joan Tate (London: Longmans, Green and Co., 1966), 23, 29.

p. 5, *As musician and activist impact investor Bono commented…* Andrew Ross Sorkin, "A New Fund Seeks Both Financial and Social Returns," *New York Times,* December 19, 2016, https://www.nytimes.com/2016/12/19/business/dealbook/a-new-fund-seeks-both-financial-and-social-returns.html.

Chapter 1 The Founders

p. 7, *"the corn and hog capital of the world"* … Lee Gutkind, *Many Sleepless Nights: The World of Organ Transplantation* (Pittsburgh: University of Pittsburgh Press, 1990), 42.

p. 7, *Starting in the late 1920s…* Thomas E. Starzl, *The Puzzle People: Memoirs of a Transplant Surgeon* (Pittsburgh: University of Pittsburg Press, 1992), 10.

p. 8, *Moving on from dreaming up new worlds…* Starzl, *Puzzle People,* 13.

p. 8, *R. F.'s second son, Tom…* Starzl, *Puzzle People,* 22.

p. 8, *"The barrage of ridicule and criticism…"* Gutkind, *Many Sleepless Nights,* 48.

p. 8, *During his tenure in Pittsburgh, Dr. Starzl…* Gutkind, *Many Sleepless Nights,* 43–44.

p. 9, *"The man is an enigma"…* Gutkind, *Many Sleepless Nights,* 42.

p. 9, *Dr. Starzl also emerged as a prolific medical author…* University of Pittsburgh Medical Center, "Thomas E. Starzl, MD, PhD," http://www.upmc.com/media/experts/pages/thomas-e-starzl.aspx.

p. 9, …*"the Father of Modern Transplantation"* University of Pittsburgh Medical Center, "Thomas E. Starzl, MD, PhD."

p. 11, *Today it's a part of Alere...* In February 2016, Alere agreed to be acquired by Abbott for an expected $5.8 billion. Leslie Picker, "Abbott to Acquire Alere, a Maker of Medical Diagnostics Tests," *New York Times*, February 1, 2016, http://www.nytimes.com/2016/02/02/business/dealbook/abbott-to-acquire-alere-a-maker-of-medical-tests.html.

Chapter 2   An Unlikely Intervention

p. 18, *...this movement actually signifies something closer to agreement...* Sharell Cook, "What Is the Meaning of the Indian Head Shake?: The Indian Head Wobble Demystified," TripSavvy, http://goindia.about.com/od/greetingscommunication/a/head-wobble.htm.

p. 18, *Despite India's increasing prosperity and economic vitality...* UNICEF, *Committing to Child Survival: A Promise Renewed: Progress Report 2012*, September 2012, https://www.unicef.org/eapro/A_Promise_Renewed_Report_2012.pdf.

p. 18, *Unfortunately, these were of limited value...* World Health Organization, "WHO's First Global Report on Antibiotic Resistance Reveals Serious, Worldwide Threat to Public Health," April 30, 2014, http://www.who.int/mediacentre/news/releases/2014/amr-report/en. The report concludes, "Antibiotic resistance—when bacteria change so antibiotics no longer work in people who need them to treat infections—is now a major threat to public health." See also Maryn McKenna, "World Health Organization: Antibiotic Resistance Grave Global Problem," *Wired*, May 5, 2014, http://www.wired.com/2014/05/who-amr-report.

p. 18, *"Is this an absolutely impossible problem..."* Late in his life, Tim's father, Dr. Thomas Starzl, described a similar focus when he began his career as an organ transplant surgeon, asking himself, "What's out there that needs development but looks impossible?" James R. Hagerty, "'Father of Transplantation' Defeated His

Own Doubts," *Wall Street Journal*, March 18-19, 2017, A10.

p. 20, *A particularly important antibody...* Andrew M. Keech, *Peptide Immunotherapy: Colostrum, A Physician's Reference Guide* (AKS Publishing, 2009), 39, 204–205.

p. 20, *...it would allow him to apply the term "patent pending"...* United States Patent and Trademark Office, *Provisional Application for Patent,* http://www.uspto.gov/patents-getting-started/patent-basics/types-patent-applications/provisional-application-patent.

p. 22, *In fact, Dr. Nash believed such a product might be effective as a prophylactic...* Dr. Peter Nash, telephone interview by author, December 1, 2010.

p. 23, *...international companies had been accused in the past of endangering the health of children...* Stephen Solomon, "The Controversy over Infant Formula," *New York Times Magazine,* December 6, 1981, http://www.nytimes.com/1981/12/06/magazine/the-controversy-over-infant-formula.html.

p. 24, *By the time children arrived...* "Fresh Cases of Diarrhoea Reported Daily in Doon with Rise in Temperature," *Dehradun Daily Pioneer,* May 9, 2013; "Humidity Proves Fatal for Doon, DVD Cases Up," *Dehradun Daily Pioneer*, May 26, 2013; "Patients Surge at Doon Hospital as OPD Reopens," *DehradunBuzz.com,* February 1, 2012.

p. 25, *India's drug market...* Adi Narayan, "Welcome to India, the Land of the Drug Reps," *Bloomberg Business Week,* September 12–18, 2011, 26.

p. 25, *... an estimated 20 percent of the drugs sold in India...* Gardiner Harris, "Medicines Made in India Set Off Safety Worries," *New York Times,* February 14, 2014, http://www.nytimes.com/2014/02/15/world/asia/medicines-made-in-india-set-off-safety-worries.html?nl=todaysheadlines&emc=edit_th_20140215.

p. 25, *One study in New Delhi...* "Fake Drugs Being Offered for Cheaper Rates: Survey," *The Hindu,* May 21, 2010.

Chapter 3   The Leather Apron Club

p. 31, *Over 90 percent of startups fail...* Startup Genome, "Startup Genome Report Extra on Premature Scaling: A Deep Dive into Why Most High Growth Startups Fail," 2011, http://s3.amazonaws.com/ startupcompass-public/StartupGenomeReport2_Why_Startups_ Fail_v2.pdf, 4.

p. 33, *...Food and Drug Administration (FDA) approval...* For a detailed description of the clinical trial and drug approval process, see Center for Global Development, *Safer, Faster, Cheaper: Improving Clinical Trials and Regulatory Pathways to Fight Neglected Diseases* (Washington, D.C., 2011), 7-10

p. 35, *...a "social impact" or "double bottom line" investment opportunity...* "Philanthropy Meets the Market," *The World in 2014* (*The Economist* special issue, 2013), 82.

p. 35, *In his biography of the Founding Father...* Walter Isaacson, "The America Ben Franklin Saw," *Washington Post*, November 21, 2012, https://www.washingtonpost.com/opinions/walter-isaacson-the-america-ben-franklin-saw/2012/11/21/8094bfca-3411-11e2-bfd5-e202b6d7b501_story.html?noredirect=on&utm_term=.cc327a46b01.

p. 35, *In May 2012, The Economist described...* "Spreading Gospels of Wealth: America's Billionaire Giving Pledgers Are Forming a Movement," *The Economist*, May 19, 2012, http://www.economist.com/ node/21555605.

p. 36, *"I think it's tough to serve two masters..."* David Blank, "Bill Gates Is Putting His Own Money into a Small Impact-Investing Fund Focused on India," *Quartz*, November 16, 2014, http://qz.com/297097/ bill-gates-unitus-seee-fund-impact-investing-fund-focused-on-india.

p. 36, *In March 2014, "an elite group..."* Jamie Johnson, "Including the Young and the Rich: White House Hosts 'Next Generation' Young and Rich," *New York Times*, April 20, 2014.

Chapter 4   A Neglected Disease

p. 39, *By 2010 diarrhea was the second leading cause of death...* Bill and Melinda Gates Foundation, "What We Do: Enteric and Diarrheal Diseases: Strategy Overview," http://www.gatesfoundation.org/What-We-Do/Global-Health/Enteric-and-Diarrheal-Diseases.

p. 40, *As staggering as these numbers are...* Sara M. Bartsch and Bruce Y. Lee, "Economics and Financing of Vaccines for Diarrheal Diseases," *Human Vaccines & Immunotherapeutics* 10, no. 6 (June 1, 2014): 1568-81.

p. 40, *Indeed, fewer than half of all deaths globally...* Paul H. Wise and Gary L. Darmstadt, "The Grand Divergence in Global Child Health: Confronting Data Requirements in Areas of Conflict and Chronic Instability," *JAMA Pediatrics* 170, no. 3 (2016): 195-97, doi: 10.1001/jamapediatrics.2015.4275.

p. 40, *...of the estimated nine million individuals who die in India every year...* Cathy Edwards and Suhail Haleem, "The Mystery of India's Unrecorded Deaths," *BBC*, July 12, 2014, http://www.bbc.com/news/health-28228177.

p. 40, *Meanwhile, though the official statistics have slowly improved...* Christa L. Fischer Walker et al., "Global Burden of Childhood Pneumonia and Diarrhoea," *The Lancet* 381 no. 9876 (April 20, 2013): 1405–16; Elizabeth D. Gibbons, "Climate Change, Children's Rights, and the Pursuit of Intergenerational Climate Justice," *Health and Human Rights Journal* 16, no. 1 (June 2014): 19–31.

p. 40, *Studies suggest that the number of malnourished children...* Gibbons, "Climate Change, Children's Rights, and the Pursuit of Intergenerational Climate Justice," 21.

p. 40, *Imagine a city in the United States...* During the period in which this book was being written, a crisis comparable to the hypothetical example suggested in the text, and the ensuing public and governmental outrage, occurred when a change in the source of water supplied to homes in Flint, Michigan, created unacceptable levels of lead in the city's drinking water. See "Events That Led to Flint's Water Crisis," *New York Times*, January 21, 2016, http://www.nytimes.com/interactive/2016/01/21/us/flint-lead-water-timeline.html; MSNBC, "Flint Water Crisis: A Timeline," January 27, 2016, http://www.msnbc.com/msnbc/flint-water-crisis-timeline.

p. 41, *This disparity was highlighted by UNICEF...* UNICEF, *Pneumonia and Diarrhea: Tackling the Deadliest Diseases for the World's Poorest Children,* June 2012, http://www.unicef.org/media/files/UNICEF_P_D_complete_0604.pdf.

p. 41, *While the UNICEF report acknowledged...* UNICEF, *Pneumonia and Diarrhea.*

p. 41, *Approximately half of these cases are caused by noroviruses...* Herbert L. DuPont, "Acute Infectious Diarrhea in Immunocompetent Adults," *New England Journal of Medicine* 370 (2014): 1532–40.

p. 41, *The health-care costs associated with norovirus cases...* Bartsch and Lee, "Economics and Financing of Vaccines for Diarrheal Diseases."

p. 42, *As many as 10 million international travelers...* Herbert L. DuPont and Fida M. Khan, "Travelers' Diarrhea: Epidemiology, Microbiology, Prevention, and Therapy," *Journal of Travel Medicine* 1, no. 2 (June 1, 1994): 84-93.

p. 42, *Studies suggest that over 60 percent of travelers...* Morteza Izadi and Afshin Sadepur, "A Closer Look to the Most Frequent Travelers' Disease: A Systematic Update on Travelers' Diarrhea," *International Journal of Travel Medicine and Global Health* 2, no. 3 (2014): 95–99.

p. 42, *Prior to World War II and the introduction of antibiotics...* William Firshein, *The Infectious Microbe* (New York: Oxford University Press, 2014), Kindle edition, loc. 232; Jared Diamond, *Guns, Germs, and Steel* (New York and London: W. W. Norton & Company, 1997), 189.

p. 42, *Nearly 45,000 Union soldiers...* Matthew L. Lim et al., "History of U.S. Military Contributions to the Study of Diarrheal Diseases," *Military Medicine* 170, no. 4 (2005): 30-38; Henschen, *History of Diseases*, 75.

p. 43, *The approximately two million military personnel...* See also J. Heggers, "Microbial Invasion: The Major Ally of War," *Military Medicine* 143 (1978): 390–94; K.C. Hyams et al., "Diarrheal Disease during Operation Desert Shield," *New England Journal of Medicine* 325 (1991): 1423–28.

p. 43, *The Global Enteric Multicenter Study (GEMS)...* Karen L. Kotloff et al., "Burden and Etiology of Diarrhoeal Disease in Infants and Young Children in Developing Countries (the Global Enteric Multicenter Study, GEMS): A Prospective, Case-Control Study," *The Lancet* 382, no. 9888 (July 20, 2013): 209–22.

p. 44, *Rotavirus, the leading cause...* A. K. Siddique et al., "Epidemiology of Rotavirus and Cholera in Children Aged Less than Five Years in Rural Bangladesh," *Journal of Health, Population and Nutrition* 29, no. 1 (February 2011): 1–8.

p. 44, *Studies have shown that during the first two years of life...* Walker et al., "Global Burden of Childhood Pneumonia and Diarrhoea." In India, stunting affects even the country's richest families. See Gardiner Harris, "Poor Sanitation in India May Afflict Well-Fed Children With Malnutrition," *New York Times,* July 13, 2014, http://www.nytimes.com/2014/07/15/world/asia/poor-sanitation-in-india-may-afflict-well-fed-children-with-malnutrition.html.

p. 44, *Affecting approximately 162 million children around the globe...* World Health Organization, "Global Nutrition Targets 2025: Stunting Policy Brief," (Geneva: World Health Organization, 2014).

p. 44, *Stunted children grow up to have...* World Health Organization, "Global Nutrition Targets 2025: Stunting Policy Brief."

p. 45, *The GEMS study confirmed earlier studies...* Kotloff, "Burden and Etiology of Diarrhoeal Disease."

p. 45, *WHO has reported that 50 percent...* PATH, "In-depth: Why Isn't Oral Rehydration Solution Defeating Diarrheal Disease?," http://sites.path.org/drugdevelopment/2015/03/in-depth-why-isnt-oral-rehydration-solution-defeating-diarrheal-disease/.

p. 45, *Malnutrition is the cause of 53 percent...* Laura E. Caulfield, Mercedes de Onis, Monika Blössner, and Robert E. Black, "Undernutrition as an Underlying Cause of Child Deaths Associated with Diarrhea, Pneumonia, Malaria, and Measles," *American Journal of Clinical Nutrition* 80, no. 1 (2004): 193–98.

p. 45, *Malnutrition weakens the child's immune system...* Rebecca J. Scharf, Mark D. DeBoer, and Richard L. Guerrant, "Recent Advances in Understanding the Long-Term Sequelae of Childhood Infectious Diarrhea," *Current Infectious Diseases Report* 16, no. 6 (2014).

p. 45, *Recent studies show these long-term effects...* Scharf, DeBoer, and Guerrant, "Recent Advances in Understanding the Long-Term Sequelae of Childhood Infectious Diarrhea," 4.

p. 45, *Diarrhea also has an economic cost...* Water and Sanitation Program, *The Economic Impacts of Inadequate Sanitation in Bangladesh,* 2012, https://openknowledge.worldbank.org/bitstream/handle/10986/17349/717330WP0Box370SI0Bangladesh0Report.pdf; Water and Sanitation Program, *The Economic Impacts of Inadequate Sanitation in India,* 2011, http://documents.worldbank.org/curated/en/820131468041640929/pdf/681590WSP0Box30UBLIC00WSP0esi0india.pdf.

p. 46, *A 2008 study in India...* Rachel M. Burke et al., "The Burden of Pediatric Diarrhea: A Cross-Sectional Study of Incurred Costs and Perceptions of Cost among Bolivian Families," *BMC Public Health* 13, no. 708 (2013): 2, https://bmcpublichealth.biomedcentral.com/track/pdf/10.1186/1471-2458-13-708.

p. 46, *A similar 2013 study in Bolivia...* Burke et al., "The Burden of Pediatric Diarrhea," 8.

p. 46, *Interventions to improve water quality in underdeveloped countries...*
Zulfiqar A. Bhutta et al., "Interventions to Address Deaths from
Childhood Pneumonia and Diarrhea Equitably: What Works and at
What Cost?," *The Lancet* 381, no. 9875 (April 20, 2013): 1417–29.

p. 46, *Even with such progress...* UNICEF and WHO, *Progress on Sanitation
and Drinking Water: 2015 Update and MDG Assessment,* 2015,
https://washdata.org/sites/default/files/documents/reports/2017-
06/JMP-2015-Report.pdf. See also Guy Hutton, "Global Costs
and Benefits of Drinking-Water Supply and Sanitation
Interventions to Reach the MDG Target and Universal Coverage,"
(Geneva: World Health Organization, 2012).

p. 46, *Nowhere is this more apparent than in India...* See Harris, "Poor
Sanitation in India."

p. 47, *"We are in the twenty-first century..."* Abhaya Srivastava, "New
Village Toilets a Small Step for Poor Indian Women," *Business
Insider,* August 31, 2014, http://www.businessinsider.com/
afp-new-village-toilets-a-small-step-for-poor-indian-women-2014-8.

p. 47, *The project, Clean India...* Bill Gates, "India Is Winning Its War
on Human Waste," Gatesnotes blog, April 25, 2017, https://www.
gatesnotes.com/Development/Indias-War-on-Human-Waste. See
also Niharika Mandhana, "Going Outside Turns Political in India
Toilet Drive," *Wall Street Journal,* February 10, 2017, https://www.
wsj.com/articles/going-outside-turns-political-in-india-toilet-
drive-1486722604.

p. 47, *WHO studies suggest...* Hutton, "Global Costs and Benefits of
Drinking-Water Supply and Sanitation Interventions." See also David
Bornstein, "The Real Future of Clean Water," *New York Times,*
August 21, 2013, http://opinionator.blogs.nytimes.com/2013/08/21/
the-real-future-of-clean-water.

p. 47, *The Bill and Melinda Gates Foundation...* Bill and Melinda Gates
Foundation, "What We Do: Enteric and Diarrheal Diseases:

Strategy Overview." A cholera vaccine called Shanchol has proven to be highly effective in a very large-scale clinical trial conducted by icddr,b in Dhaka, Bangladesh, and funded by the Gates Foundation. Firdausi Qadri et al., "Feasibility and Effectiveness of Oral Cholera Vaccine in an Urban Endemic Setting in Bangladesh: A Cluster Randomised Open-Label Trial," *The Lancet,* 386, no. 10001 (October 3, 2015): 1362-71.

p. 48, *Four vaccines for rotavirus*...The vaccines are Rotarix (GlaxoSmithKline), RotaTeq (Merck and Co., Inc.), Rotasil (Serum Institute of India), and Rotavac (Bharat BioTech). Donald G. McNeil Jr., "New Vaccine Could Slow Disease That Kills 600 Children a Day," *New York Times,* March 22, 2017, https://www.nytimes.com/2017/03/22/health/rotavirus vaccine.html.

p. 48, *Underdeveloped countries also pose challenges*... Leila A. Haidari et al., "Augmenting Transport versus Increasing Cold Storage to Improve Vaccine Supply Chains," *PLOS ONE* 8, no. 5 (May 22, 2013), http://www.plosone.org/article/info%3Adoi%2F10.1371%2Fjournal.pone.0064303.

p. 48, *Electricity is either unavailable or erratic*... Another cause of blackouts in India is the widespread theft of electricity. It is estimated that more than 25 percent of India's power is squandered because of theft and inadequate wiring. Rakteem Katakey and Rajesh Kumar Singh, "India Fights to Keep the Lights On," *Bloomberg Businessweek,* June 5, 2014, 22.

p. 49, *"Can you name a miracle food..."* Nicholas D. Kristof, "A Free Miracle Food!," *New York Times,* July 10, 2013, http://www.nytimes.com/2013/07/11/opinion/kristof-a-free-miracle-food.html.

p. 49, *The immunological, economic, social, psychological, and environmental benefits*... Bhutta et al., "Interventions to Address Deaths from Childhood Pneumonia and Diarrhea Equitably."

p. 49, *One recent study conducted over a 30-year period*... Cesar G. Victora et al.,

"Association between Breastfeeding and Intelligence, Educational Attainment, and Income at 30 Years of Age: A Prospective Birth Cohort Study from Brazil," *The Lancet Global Health* 3, no. 4 (April 2015): e199–e205.

p. 50, *Marginal breastfeeding results...* Cesar G. Victora et al., "Breastfeeding in the 21st Century: Epidemiology, Mechanisms, and Lifelong Effect," *The Lancet* 387, no. 10017 (January 30, 2016): 475–90.

p. 50, *Even in the United States...* Ana Francisca Diallo, "Assessing the Impact of Breastfeeding Cessation on the Reported Incidence of Diarrhea in Infants Between the Ages of 7 to 12 months: A Secondary Data Analysis," University of Connecticut, master's thesis, 2016, http://digitalcommons.uconn.edu/gs_theses/1019.

p. 50, *The human gut...* Firshein, *The Infectious Microbe*, Kindle edition, loc. 180–94.

p. 50, *...are called "probiotics."* FAO/WHO, ed., *Guidelines for the Evaluation of Probiotics in Food*, 2002, http://www.who.int/foodsafety/fs_management/en/probiotic_guidelines.pdf. See also C. Hill et al., "Expert Consensus Document: The International Scientific Association for Probiotics and Prebiotics Consensus Statement on the Scope and Appropriate Use of the Term Probiotic," *Nature Reviews Gastroenterology & Hepatology* 11, no. 8 (2014): 506–14.

p. 50, *The growing fascination with functional food products...* Jane E. Brody, "Probiotic Logic vs. Gut Feelings," *New York Times,* July 21, 2014, http://well.blogs.nytimes.com/2014/07/21/probiotic-logic-vs-gut-feelings.

p. 50, *"... interest in products containing probiotics."* Grand View Research, *Probiotics Market Size, Share & Trends Analysis Report By Application (Food & Beverages, Dietary Supplements, Animal Feed), By End-use, By Region, And Segment Forecast, 2014-2024*, 2018, https://www.grandviewresearch.com/industry-analysis/probiotics-market.

p. 51, *... "the findings were mixed."* Mark Manary et al., "Systematic Review of the Care of Children with Diarrhoea in the Community-Based Management of Severe Acute Malnutrition," World Health Organization, February 2012.

p. 51, *Diarrhea has been designated a "neglected disease"...* Center for Global Development, *Safer, Faster, Cheaper*, 1.

p. 51, *The cost to a pharmaceutical company...* Jerry Avorn, "The $2.6 Billion Pill: Methodologic and Policy Considerations," *New England Journal of Medicine* 372 (May 14, 2015): 1877–79, doi: 10.1056/NEJM p1500848.

p. 52, *... "drug development for neglected diseases may often be just as expensive and uncertain..."* Center for Global Development, *Safer, Faster, Cheaper*, 2.

p. 52, *"Why consider researching a vaccine..."* Charles Kenny, *Getting Better: Why Global Development Is Succeeding—And How We Can Improve the World Even More* (New York: Basic Books, 2013), Kindle edition, loc. 2747.

p. 52, *Designating diarrhea as one of 30 "neglected diseases"...* Kotloff et al., "Burden and Etiology of Diarrhoeal Disease."

p. 52, *The studies concluded that potential cures...* Kotloff et al., "Burden and Etiology of Diarrhoeal Disease." See also Scharf, DeBoer, and Guerrant, "Recent Advances in Understanding the Long-Term Sequelae of Childhood Infectious Diarrhea."

p. 52, *Another study surveyed all new therapeutic products...* Kotloff et al., "Burden and Etiology of Diarrhoeal Disease."

p. 53, *These discoveries emerged from the Pakistan-SEATO Cholera Research Laboratory...* A. Mushtaque, R. Chowdhury, and Richard A. Cash, *A Simple Solution: Teaching Millions to Treat Diarrhea at Home* (Dhaka, Bangladesh: The University Press Limited, 2007), 17–22.

p. 53, icddr,b http://www.icddrb.org.

p. 53, *By the late 1960s, scientists at icddr,b...* Lin Lin Ginzberg, "The Man Who Helped Save 50 Million Lives," *BBC*, August 3, 2014, http://www.bbc.com/news/health-28564607.

p. 54, *The administration of ORS beginning at the early stages of a diarrhea episode...* Bhutta et al., "Interventions to Address Deaths from Childhood Pneumonia and Diarrhea Equitably."

p. 54, ... *"potentially the most important medical advance"...* UNICEF, "ORS: The medical advance of the century," http://www.unicef.org/sowc96/joral.htm

p. 54, *In 2001, the Gates Foundation gave icddr,b...* icddr,b, "History," http://www.icddrb.org/about-us/history.

p. 55, *According to PATH...* PATH, "In-depth: Why Isn't Oral Rehydration Solution Defeating Diarrheal Disease?"

p. 55, *PATH reports that...* PATH, "In-depth: Why Isn't Oral Rehydration Solution Defeating Diarrheal Disease?"

p. 55, *Dr. Atul Gawande...* Atul Gawande, "Slow Ideas: Some Innovations Spread Fast. How Do You Speed the Ones That Don't?," *New Yorker,* July 29, 2013, https://www.newyorker.com/magazine/2013/07/29/slow-ideas.

p. 55, *A broad survey encompassing 45 countries...* Kenney, *Getting Better,* 129.

p. 56, *A 1998 study at icddr,b...* Shafiqul A. Sarker et al., "Successful Treatment of Rotavirus Diarrhea in Children with Immunoglobulin from Immunized Bovine Colostrum," *Pediatric Infectious Disease Journal* 17, no. 12 (1998): 1149–54.

p. 56, *Experts around the globe have repeatedly avowed...* Donald G. McNeil Jr., "A Quiet Revolution in the Treatment of Childhood Diarrhea," *New York Times,* August 10, 2015, http://www.nytimes.com/2015/08/11/health/catching-up-with-a-childhood-killer-diarrhea.html.

Chapter 5 "Comparable Results"

p. 60, *The region encompassing Dehradun and Meerut...* "India Leopard on Loose Causes Panic in Meerut Town," *BBC,* February 24, 2014,

http://www.bbc.com/news/world-asia-india-26319400.

p. 61, Tara Child Care Center http://www.tarachildcare.com.

Chapter 6   Boulder

p. 69, *In Startup Communities...* Brad Feld, *Startup Communities: Building an Entrepreneurial Ecosystem in Your City* (Hoboken, NJ: John Wiley & Sons, 2012).

p. 69, *By 1976, Celestial...* Frank W. Martin, "Mo Siegel Was Blending Red Zinger when He Knew Celestial Seasonings Was His Cup of Tea," *People* 6, no. 11 (September 13, 1976).

p. 71, *He was drawn to the University of Michigan...* In May 2014, Mark Braman was inducted into the Midland County Sports Hall of Fame. Dan Chalk, "Braman Started 24 Straight Games for U-M football," *Midland Daily News,* May 2, 2014.

Chapter 7   The New Team

p. 87, *Another concern: India's health-care system includes...* "Quackdown: The High Cost of Medicines Bought on the Cheap," *The Economist,* February 21, 2008, http://www.economist.com/node/10727817.

p. 88, APS BioGroup http://apsbiogroup.com/colostrum.

p. 91, *...Teenage Mutant Ninja Turtles...* Harvey R. Greenberg, "Just How Powerful Are Those Turtles?," *New York Times,* April 15, 1990, http://www.nytimes.com/1990/04/15/movies/just-how-powerful-are-those-turtles.html; Jennifer 8. Lee, "Heroes in a Half Shell Turn the Big 2-5," *New York Times,* April 20, 2009, http://cityroom.blogs.nytimes.com/2009/04/20/heroes-n-a-half-shell-turn-the-big-2-5.

Chapter 8 India Impasse

p. 94, *The UNICEF report highlights India...* UNICEF, *Committing to Child Survival: A Promise Renewed: Progress Report 2012*. Margherita Stancati, "Almost 5,000 Indian Children Die Daily," *Wall Street Journal*, September 13, 2012.

p. 95, *The prestigious Singapore-based Political and Economic Risk Consultancy issued a report...* "Indian Bureaucracy Rated Worst in Asia, Says a Political & Economic Risk Consultancy Report," *Economic Times*, January 11, 2012, https://economictimes.indiatimes.com/news/politics-and-nation/indian-bureaucracy-rated-worst-in-asia-says-a-political-economic-risk-consultancy-report/articleshow/11447261.cms.

p. 95, *"Corruption has become such an endemic feature..."* Jean Drèze and Amartya Sen, *An Uncertain Glory: India and Its Contradictions* (Princeton, NJ: Princeton University Press, 2013), 93.

p. 95, *The result is a toxic culture...* Drèze and Sen, *An Uncertain Glory*, 95–96.

p. 100, *In October 2013, the New York Times reported that Wal-Mart...* Gardiner Harris, "Wal-Mart Drops Ambitious Expansion Plan for India," *New York Times*, October 9, 2013.

Chapter 9 Bangladesh

p. 103, *One Indian diplomat concluded...* Gary J. Bass, *The Blood Telegram* (New York: Alfred A. Knopf, 2013), Kindle edition loc. 607.

p. 103, icddr,b http://www.icddrb.org.

p. 103, *"Once we developed a method..."* Amy Yee, "Profile: The icddr,b— Saving Lives in Bangladesh and Beyond," *The Lancet* 381, no. 9875 (April 20, 2013): 1350.

p. 104, *Dr. Mahalanabis later recalled...* "A Simple Solution," *Time*, October 16, 2006, 44.

p. 104, *In the 1980s, a nongovernmental organization...* Mushtaque,

Chowdhury, and Cash, *A Simple Solution,* 39–61.

p. 104, … *"one of the great mysteries of global health."* Pamela Das and Richard Horton, "Bangladesh: Innovating for Health," *The Lancet* 382, no. 9906 (November 23, 2013): 1681.

p. 104, *"The most dramatic period of improvement…"* "The Path through the Fields," *The Economist,* November 3, 2012, https://www.economist.com/news/briefing/21565617-bangladesh-has-dysfunctional-politics-and-stunted-private-sector-yet-it-has-been-surprisingly.

p. 105, *Indeed, although it remains one of the poorest countries in the world…* Drèze and Sen, *An Uncertain Glory,* 54.

p. 105, *In a revealing series of articles in November 2013…* A. Mushtaque et al., "The Bangladesh Paradox: Exceptional Health Achievement Despite Economic Poverty," *The Lancet* 382, no. 9906 (November 23, 2013): 1734–45.

p. 105, *This trend was accompanied by the emergence…* Christopher J. Gil et al., "Bottlenecks, Barriers, and Solutions: Results from Multicounty Consultations Focused on Reduction of Childhood Pneumonia and Diarrhea Deaths," *The Lancet* 381, no. 9876 (April 27, 2013): 1487–98.

Chapter 10   The Bangladesh Trial

p. 108, PATH http://www.path.org/about/index.php.

p. 108, *In August 2011, Simpson had identified icddr,b…* Telephone conference with Evan Simpson, August 9, 2011.

p. 108, icddr,b http://www.icddrb.org.

p. 108, *With over 15 million residents…* "Does Dhaka Need Rickshaws?," *BBC,* July 20, 1998, http://news.bbc.co.uk/2/hi/south_asia/136074.stm; "Dangers in Dhaka, the World's Fastest-Growing City," *BBC,* July 7, 2010, http://www.bbc.co.uk/news/10542218.

p. 108, *Unremitting traffic jams…* Michael Hobbes, "Lessons from the Traffic Capital of the World," *New Republic,* July 14, 2014.

p. 108, *Lacking access to transport...* Hobbes, "Lessons from the Traffic Capital of the World."

p. 108, *The number of inhabitants in the slums of the city...* Gardiner Harris, "Borrowed Time on Disappearing Land: Facing Rising Seas, Bangladesh Confronts the Consequences of Climate Change," *New York Times,* March 28, 2014.

p. 109, *Evan Simpson was aware that Dr. Sarker had published...* Sarker et al., "Successful Treatment of Rotavirus Diarrhea." Shafiqul A. Sarker et al., "Randomized, Placebo-Controlled, Clinical Trial of Hyperimmunized Chicken Egg Yolk Immunoglobulin in Children with Rotavirus Diarrhea," *Journal of Pediatric Gastroenterology and Nutrition* 32, no. 1 (January 2001): 19–25.

p. 113, *The Bangladesh garment industry...* Ferdous Ahamed, "Improving Social Compliance in Bangladesh's Ready-made Garment Industry," *Labour and Management in Development* 13 (2012): 1-26.

p. 113, *... "strike culture"* Patrick Barta and Syed Zain Al-Mahmood, "Culture of Mass Strikes Suffocates Bangladesh's Economy," *Wall Street Journal,* August 3-4, 2013, A7.

p. 113, *"This is Bangladesh..."* M. Shamsur Rabb Khan, "A Country of Hartals," *Daily Star,* April 11, 2013.

p. 114, *It was at this point, right after a two-week truce...* Jim Yardley and Julfikar Ali Manik, "Anti-blasphemy Protests in Bangladesh Turn Violent," *New York Times,* May 6, 2013, https://www.nytimes. com/2013/05/07/world/asia/two-days-of-riots-in-bangladesh- turn-deadly.html.

p. 114, *As the situation worsened...* Dr. Sarker was not alone in suggesting ambulances as the preferred mode of transportation. The *Wall Street Journal* reported, "Some businessmen go to extremes during hartals—including hiring private ambulances for about $150 a day to move safely through the streets." Barta and Al-Mahmood, "Culture of Mass Strikes Suffocates Bangladesh's Economy."

p. 116, *...coinciding with another violent strike...* "Two Killed, 3 Drivers Burnt: Brutality Mark Jamaat's Second Day of Hartal," *Daily Star,* September 20, 2013.

Chapter 11   Staying the Course

p. 122, Project C.U.R.E. https://projectcure.org.

p. 125, *A close observer of Dr. Thomas Starzl...* Gutkind, *Many Sleepless Nights,* 365.

p. 127, *The placebo used in a double-blind clinical study...* "One Scholar's Take on the Power of the Placebo," NPR interview with Dr. Ted Kaptchuk, January 6, 2012, http://www.npr.org/2012/01/06/144794035/one-scholars-take-on-the-power-of-the-placebo.

p. 127, *...in many instances patients experience beneficial effects from placebo*s... Richard Knox, "Half of a Drug's Power Comes from Thinking It Will Work," NPR, January 10, 2014, http://www.npr.org/blogs/health/2014/01/10/261406721/half-a-drugs-power-comes-from-thinking-it-will-work.

Chapter 12   The Elephant in the Room

p. 132, *The obituary in the Denver Post observed...* "Craig Johnson: Obituary," *Denver Post,* January 12, 2014.

p. 133, *In order to participate in the economic opportunities...* Suzanne Elvidge, "Emerging Markets and Your Global Regulatory Strategy," *Pharmaceutical Online,* November 27, 2013, http://www.pharmaceuticalonline.com/doc/emerging-markets-and-your-global-regulatory-strategy-0001.

p. 133, *The concept of harmonizing regulatory schemes...* Institute of Medicine, *International Regulatory Harmonization amid Globalization of Drug Development: Workshop Summary,* (Washington, DC: National Academies Press, 2013).

p. 135, *The largest inland port in the United States...* James Carafano (@ JJCarafano), "A View from the Border," Twitter post, October 31, 2011; "Written testimony of U.S. Customs and Border Protection Office of Field Operations—Laredo Field Office, Director of Field Operations Gene Garza for a House Committee on Homeland Security, Subcommittee on Border and Maritime Security field hearing titled 'Using Technology to Facilitate Trade and Enhance Security at Our Ports of Entry,'" May 1, 2012, https://www.dhs.gov/news/2012/05/01/written-testimony-us-customs-and-border-protection-house-homeland-security.

p. 139, *Dr. Reddy's Laboratories...* Gauri Kamath, "Dr. Kallam Anji Reddy: The Man Who Introduced India to the Drug Called Innovation," *Economic Times,* May 17, 2013, https://economictimes.indiatimes.com/news/company/corporate-trends/dr-kallam-anji-reddy-the-man-who-introduced-india-to-the-drug-called-innova-tion/articleshow/19009383.cms.

p. 139, *Although his parents had...* K. Anji Reddy, *An Unfinished Agenda: My Life in the Pharmaceuticals Industry* (London: Penguin Books, 2015).

p. 141, *"It's going to create a certain sense of stability..."* Wendy Koch, "India More Appealing to U.S., Firms Expect Stable Climate," *USA Today,* May 19, 2014, B1.

p. 143, *The program, known as Innovation Countdown 2030...* Amie Batson, "How to Accelerate Innovation to Solve the World's Most Urgent Health Issues," Innovation Countdown 2030, July 12, 2015, http://ic2030.org/2015/07/accelerate-innovation.

p. 145, *According to the FDA, the primary objective of the IRB process...* U.S. Food & Drug Administration, "Institutional Review Boards Frequently Asked Questions—Information Sheet," http://www.fda.gov/RegulatoryInformation/Guidances/ucm126420.htm.

Chapter 13　A Strategic Inflection Point

p. 148, *Andy Grove, the legendary co-founder...* Andrew S. Grove, *Only the Paranoid Survive: How to Exploit the Crisis Points that Challenge Every Company and Career* (New York: Doubleday, 1996), 3.

p. 148, *Grove argued that "a strategic inflection point..."* Grove, *Only the Paranoid Survive*, 28.

p. 149, *...the U.S. alone has over 190 egg-producing companies...* The American Egg Board, "Check Out the Latest Facts on the Egg Business," accessed September 1, 2016, http://www.aeb.org/ farmers-and-marketers/industry-overview.

p. 149, *..."nature's perfect first food."* Andrew Keech, "Colostrum: Nature's Perfect Food for Infants and Adults," Foundation for Alternative and Integrative Medicine, http://www.faim.org/ colostrum-natures-perfect-food-for-infants-and-adults.

p. 149, *However, a number of studies suggest...* Jennifer Steele et al., "Hyperimmune Bovine Colostrum for Treatment of GI Infections: A Review and Update on Clostridium Difficile," *Human Vaccines & Immunotherapeutics* 9, no. 7 (July 2013): 1565–68.

p. 149, *One study even found that colostrum could be three times more effective...* Maria Rosaria Cesarone et al., "Prevention of Influenza Episodes with Colostrum Compared with Vaccination in Healthy and High-Risk Cardiovascular Subjects: The Epidemiologic Study in San Valentino," *Clinical and Applied Thrombosis/Hemostasis* 13, no. 2 (April 2007): 130–36, doi: 10.1177/1076029606295957.

p. 149, *Bovine colostrum, reputed to contain...* Keech, "Colostrum."

p. 152, APS BioGroup http://apsbiogroup.com/colostrum.

p. 154, *Rather than employing financial engineering...* Pegasus Capital Advisors http://www.pcalp.com.

Chapter 14   Statistically Significant Efficacy

p. 164, *In December 2017, the researchers revealed the detailed results...* James T. Gaensbauer et al., "Efficacy of a Bovine Colostrum and Egg-Based Intervention in Acute Childhood Diarrhoea in Guatemala: A Randomised, Double-Blind, Placebo-Controlled Trial," *BMJ Global Health* 2, no. 4 (December 4, 2017), http://gh.bmj.com/content/2/4/e000452.

p. 165, *The study confirmed...* J. Gaensbauer et al., "Efficacy of a Novel Nutritional Product in Acute Childhood Diarrhea in Guatemala: Secondary and Exploratory Analyses of a Randomized, Double Blind, Placebo Controlled Trial," *Open Forum Infectious Diseases* 4, suppl 1 (October 1, 2017), https://academic.oup.com/ofid/article/4/suppl_1/S117/4295549/Efficacy-of-a-Novel-Nutritional-Product-in-Acute.

p. 166, *The Centers for Disease Control and Prevention estimates...* Centers for Disease Control and Prevention, "Antibiotic/Antimicrobial Resistance," https://www.cdc.gov/drugresistance/index.html.

Chapter 15   A Medical Nutrition Company

p. 175, ... *"microbes are the centre of the universe"* and *"the most significant revolution in biology since Darwin."* Ed Yong, *I Contain Multitudes: The Microbes within Us and a Grander View of Life,* (New York: HarperCollins, 2016), 20.

p. 175, ... *"revolution in science."* Anna Collen, *10% Human: How Your Body's Microbes Hold the Key to Health and Happiness* (New York: HarperCollins, 2016), 18.

p. 175, PubMed https://www.ncbi.nlm.nih.gov/pubmed.

p. 175, *Every year, the Cleveland Clinic announces...* Lydia Coutré, "Cleveland Clinic Announces Top 10 Medical Innovations for 2017," accessed September 27, 2017, http://www.crainscleveland.

com/article/20161026/NEWS/161029858/cleveland-clinic-announces-top-10-medical-innovations-for-2017.

p. 175, *In early 2017, Merriam-Webster added...* Carolyn Gregorie, "Merriam-Webster Welcomes 'Microbiome' to the English Language," *Huffington Post*, February 10, 2017, https://www.huffingtonpost.com/entry/merriam-webster-dictionary-new-word_us_589ca840e4b04061313 c18a4. The dictionary defined microbiome as a noun meaning "a community of microorganisms (such as bacteria, fungi, and viruses) that inhabit a particular environment and especially the collection of microorganisms living in or on the human body."

p. 175, *... "essential organ"* Yong, *I Contain Multitudes*, 44.

p. 175, *... "the forgotten organ, the unseen organ"* Collen, *10% Human*, 279; Sonnenburg and Sonnenburg, *The Good Gut*, 29.

p. 175, *When this organ fails to maintain the appropriate balance...* Sonnenburg and Sonnenburg, *The Good Gut*, 32.

p. 176, *... "colonization resistance."* Sonnenburg and Sonnenburg, *The Good Gut*, 165.

p. 177, *The field is so vast and complex...* Maxx Chatsko, "What the F@$! is Synthetic Biology?," Genetic Literacy Project, August 5, 2014, https://geneticliteracyproject.org/2014/08/05/what-the-f-is-synthetic-biology.

p. 178, *One definition calls it "the application..."* Chatsko, "What the F@$! is Synthetic Biology?"

p. 178, *The author of a recent best-selling book...* Yong, *I Contain Multitudes*, 239.

p. 178, *... A Simple Solution.* Mushtaque, Chowdhury, and Cash, *A Simple Solution*. See also "A Simple Solution," *Time*.

p. 179, *Nearing the end of 2017, PanTheryx...* https://pantheryx.com/equity-of-access/

p. 179, *For over 100 years before 2010,...* Jason Beaubien, "Cholera 101: Why an Ancient Disease Keeps on Haunting Us," NPR, November 4, 2016, http://www.npr.org/sections/goatsandsoda/2016/11/04/500664156/cholera-101-why-an-ancient-disease-keeps-on-haunting-us.

p. 180, *The dire situation in Haiti had been confronted...* David Whitford, "The Green Evangelist Who Scared the Energy Business Straight," *Vanity Fair*, February 21, 2017, https://www.vanityfair.com/news/2017/02/david-crane-nrg-energy.

p. 182, Project C.U.R.E. https://projectcure.org.

p. 182, *In September 2017, PanTheryx employees...* You can see a video of this event at https://vimeo.com/232065652.

p. 182, *Later that month, the company worked...* Joshua Partlow, "Strong Earthquake Shakes Mexico, Killing More Than 200 People," *Washington Post*, September 20, 2017, https://www.washingtonpost.com/world/the americas/strong-earthquake-shakes-mexico-damaging-buildings-and-causing-panic/2017/09/19/d2b044f6-9d6a-11e7-b2a7-bc70b6f98089_story.html.

p. 182, *For several decades, providing health and wellness education...* Mushtaque, Chowdhury, and Cash, *A Simple Solution,* 39–61.

p. 182, *Another is the work of WHO, UNICEF, and other organizations...* WASH in Health Care Facilities https://www.washinhcf.org/.

Selected Bibliography

Bass, Gary J. *The Blood Telegram.* New York: Alfred A. Knopf, 2013.

Collen, Anna. *10% Human: How Your Body's Microbes Hold the Key to Health and Happiness.* New York: HarperCollins, 2016.

Diamond, Jared. *Guns, Germs, and Steel.* New York and London: W. W. Norton & Company, 1997.

Drèze, Jean, and Amartya Sen. *An Uncertain Glory: India and Its Contradictions.* Princeton, NJ: Princeton University Press, 2013.

Feld, Brad. *Startup Communities: Building an Entrepreneurial Ecosystem in Your City.* Hoboken, NJ: John Wiley & Sons, 2012.

Firshein, William. *The Infectious Microbe.* New York: Oxford University Press, 2014.

Grove, Andrew S. *Only the Paranoid Survive: How to Exploit the Crisis Points that Challenge Every Company and Career.* New York: Doubleday, 1996.

Gutkind, Lee. *Many Sleepless Nights: The World of Organ Transplantation.* Pittsburgh: University of Pittsburgh Press, 1990.

Henschen, Folke. *The History of Diseases*. Trans. Joan Tate. London: Longmans, Green and Co., 1966.

Keech, Andrew M. *Peptide Immunotherapy: Colostrum, A Physician's Reference Guide*. AKS Publishing, 2009.

Kenny, Charles. *Getting Better: Why Global Development Is Succeeding—And How We Can Improve the World Even More*. New York: Basic Books, 2013.

Mushtaque, A., R. Chowdhury, and Richard A. Cash. *A Simple Solution: Teaching Millions to Treat Diarrhea at Home*. Dhaka, Bangladesh: The University Press Limited, 2007.

Reddy, K. Anji. *An Unfinished Agenda: My Life in the Pharmaceuticals Industry*. London: Penguin Books, 2015.

Sonnenburg, Justin, and Erica Sonnenburg. *The Good Gut: Taking Control of Your Weight, Your Mood, and Your Long-Term Health*. New York: Penguin Press, 2015.

Starzl, Thomas E. *The Puzzle People: Memoirs of a Transplant Surgeon*. Pittsburgh: University of Pittsburg Press, 1992.

Yong, Ed. *I Contain Multitudes: The Microbes within Us and a Grander View of Life*. New York: HarperCollins, 2016.

Index

About the Author

Tom Washing has been active in the venture capital industry for over thirty years. He is a founding partner of Sequel Venture Partners, a Colorado-based venture capital firm investing in emerging growth technology companies.

He has served on dozens of corporate and nonprofit boards of directors, including as founding Chairman of the University of Colorado Center for Entrepreneurship, President and Chairman of the Colorado Venture Capital Association, and Chairman of the Board of the University of Michigan National Technology Transfer Advisory Board. Washing was named Master Entrepreneur of the Year by the Colorado Ernst & Young Entrepreneur of the Year Awards Committee.

Washing is the co-author of the award-winning book *Passion for Skiing* (2010), and was the Assistant Film Producer of "Passion for Snow" (2013), the Emmy Award-nominated documentary film based on the book.